# "I ONLY

. . . what the Bible says," states Frances Hunter. "And the Bible says if we will ask in the name of Jesus of Nazareth, it shall be done. I believe that he performs as many miracles today as he did two thousand years ago. . . .

**"The power of God has not lessened one iota—it's there, and available for those who believe!"**

**HOT LINE TO HEAVEN is a testimony of faith and a record of fact that proves the truth of God's word: "Ye shall ask what ye will, and it will be done unto you."**

# HOT LINE TO HEAVEN

FRANCES HUNTER

published by
HUNTER MINISTRIES PUBLISHING COMPANY
1602 Townhurst
Houston, Texas 77043

Canadian Office
HUNTER MINISTRIES PUBLISHING COMPANY
OF CANADA
G-9, Station G
Calgary, Alberta, Canada T3A 2G1

## OTHER HUNTER BOOKS

*COME ALIVE*
*DELIGHTFULLY CHARISMATIC Christian*
  *Walk Seminar Manual*
*DON'T LIMIT GOD*
*FOLLOW ME*
*GOD IS FABULOUS*
*GOD'S ANSWER TO FAT . . . LOOSE IT!*
*HOW TO MAKE YOUR MARRIAGE EXCITING*
*IMPOSSIBLE MIRACLES*
*IT'S SO SIMPLE (formerly HANG LOOSE WITH JESUS)*
*LET'S GO WITNESSING (formerly GO, MAN, GO)*
*MY LOVE AFFAIR WITH CHARLES*
*NUGGETS OF TRUTH*
*P.T.L.A. (Praise the Lord, Anyway!)*
*SINCE JESUS PASSED BY*
*the fabulous SKINNIE MINNIE RECIPE BOOK*
*THIS WAY UP*
*TWO SIDES OF THE COIN*
*WHY SHOULD I SPEAK IN TONGUES*

**HOT LINE TO HEAVEN**

Copyright © 1970, By Hunter Ministries Publishing Co. All
Rights Reserved.

ISBN: 0-87162-117-7

Printed in the United States of America

DEDICATED WITH GREAT LOVE

TO MY SON TOM

*Some people accept Christ easily—they hear the gospel and don't put up a great struggle. Then there is the rebel who fights every inch of the way. Such is my son Tom.*

# CONTENTS

# CHAPTER 1

# PRAY IN FAITH BELIEVING

*And whatsoever you ask in prayer, you
will receive, if you have faith.*
—Matthew 21:22

"GOD ANSWERS the dumbest prayers for you, because
you pray the dumbest prayers in faith believing!" This
is exactly what my pastor said to me one day as I was
excitedly telling him how God had answered another
prayer. And do you know what? He was right. I was
telling him how I had asked God to deliver a gooey,
whipped cream cherry pie for me from Miami to Columbus, Ohio, *to strengthen the bonds of Christian
love.* I'm sure that God understood that whipped cream
can spoil rapidly, and that something had to move
quickly, so he just simply chartered a big Eastern Airlines jet to transport the pie for me even before it had a
chance to get warm.*

I happen to be a real nut where prayer is concerned,
because somewhere along the line I discovered that God
really answers prayer if we will only *Believe*! There are
literally hundreds of promises in the Bible concerning
prayer and yet why we fail to claim these promises I'll
never be able to understand. God promises us that if we

seek first the kingdom of God and his righteousness, all things will be ours. And how do we get what God has to offer us? By asking God. And how do we go about asking God? By prayer.

I have heard many people say, "God never answers my prayers so I quit praying." I wonder how much faith they really have. I often ask a Sunday school class on Sunday morning to share their prayer answers during the week. And do you know what? If I meet a solid brick wall and no one has had a prayer answered, then I tell them flat out that they just haven't prayed this week, because if they had prayed, there would have been some prayer answers. And if you don't believe this is true, try praying yourself.

Ask yourself honestly: Do I *really* pray? Do I really believe that God will answer prayer? Do I really pray in *faith believing*?

I want to share with you something I learned early in my Christian life. It made a very great impression upon me and I have shared it all over the United States in various churches where I've been privileged to speak. And because so many people have told me how this has affected their prayer life, I want to share it with you.

Right now I want you to do a physical thing, because this is the only way I know of to make it effective. And in the event you're not alone right now and think you might feel foolish trying this with other people watching, go jump in the bathtub (which is where I learned to pray) or hide in a closet, or lock yourself in your bedroom, but go any place where you can have privacy just to try a little experiment.

If you decided to jump in the bathtub, I hope you took the book with you so you can follow the next instructions.

1. Put your hand symbolically out toward God.
2. Straighten out your arm and reach out as far as

you possibly can. This will make sure that your hand is as far from yourself as you can physically make it.

3. Turn your palm so that it is right side up.

4. Now in your hand with the palm turned up, give God the prayer request on your heart. (If it's a *big* prayer request, you might want to cup *both* of your hands together, stretching them as far as you possibly can.) Now comes the crucial period of the prayer. What are you going to do with your hand? You have a choice of two things. You can either clench your hand and return your prayer burden to your own heart, or you can very simply follow the next step.

5. Simply turn your hand upside down so that nothing can possibly stay in your hand. Make sure that your fist isn't clenched to hold something, but stretch your fingers as far apart as possible.

6. Drop your arm to your side.

You can't bring anything back that way, can you? This is the *only* way to pray, but would you like to know that the average person prays and asks God to do something for him, and then clutches the prayer burden right back to his own little heart. And in his own strength he attempts to answer his own prayer. God says, "And whatever you ask in prayer, you will receive, *If you have faith.*"

How much faith do you have when you clutch the burden back to your own bosom? How much faith do you have when you take back the problem and try to do something about it yourself? *Give* it to God. Don't just *loan* him your prayer request; *give* it to him and then see what happens!

It's so exciting to give something to God so completely that when he answers it, you can say, "Lord, I even forgot I asked you for that because I believed so completely!"

Sometimes I feel a great urge to choke when I listen to the way some people pray, because their words really betray how little faith they have. I have heard people pray for *all* the people in their city, *all* the people in their state, *all* the people in this great country of ours, *all* the people in the world! And do you know what? They didn't believe for one minute that their prayer was going to be answered. How can you possibly pray for everyone in the world? You don't know what their needs are. God knows, to be sure, but why pray for something when you don't know what you're talking about? Did it ever dawn on you it might be better to pray for your neighbor's third toe which might be sore or broken, than to just generally pray for the whole world?

Don't you just love the beautiful-language prayer who prays to impress individuals, but whom I'm sure doesn't think about talking to God? Matthew 6:5 says "And when you pray, you must not be like the hypocrites; for they love to stand and pray in the synagogues and at the street corners, that they may be seen by men." Again in Matthew 6:7, Jesus says, "And in praying do not heap up empty phrases as the Gentiles do; for they think they will be heard for their many words."

I'm sure that God doesn't mind how we put our words together; it's only the condition of our heart that counts with him. Later on I will share with you one of the simplest, yet most eloquent, prayers I ever heard. It was dynamite, because it was sincere!

Another thing I'm sure God doesn't enjoy are the "spiritual chickens." These are the ones who preface everything with, or end with "if it be thy will." I have my own pet theory concerning this, and I hope you understand that I am not a theologian or anything of the sort. When I finally quit running from God, I came to Christ with the faith of a little child, and that's all. Agree with me or not, this is how I feel.

The day I became a Christian, I asked Christ to live his life through me. I asked to be nothing except a channel through which his mighty love could flow to reach out and touch a lost and dying world. I prayed and asked him to remove anything of my "self" or "ego" that would prevent my being the woman he wanted me to be.

Now if I believe what the Bible says; and it specifically says in Revelations 3:20, "Behold I stand at the door and knock; if any one hears my voice and opens the door, I will come in to him," then I must believe as I write, as I speak, as I actually live my life, that Christ is living his life through me. I *know* this to be a fact, because the Word of God says so. I also stand on Galatians 2:20, using the words of the great apostle Paul: "I have been crucified with Christ; it is no longer I who live, but Christ who lives in me; and the life I now live in the flesh I live by faith in the Son of God, who loved me and gave himself for me."

Therefore, if I was really sincere in asking Christ into my life, then I, too, have been crucified with Christ; it is no longer I who lives, but Christ who lives in me. Therefore, because I believe this with my heart and soul, I do not feel that a genuine Christian can pray *outside* of God's will. Would Christ pray against himself? No, he most certainly would not, and if Christ is at the very core of your being, can you pray for things that are outside of God's will?

God doesn't always answer our prayers as quickly as we think he should, but I have discovered that living my life strictly on prayer and in faith, has given me the most exciting life in the world.

Analyze your own personal prayers right now. Let me ask you a question which may seem frivolous at first, but search your very heart and soul for a truthful answer to this question: *Do you really pray?* Are your prayers just routine words you say to ease your conscience, or do you honestly and sincerely lay your life before God?

How much time do you honestly spend in prayer each day? I'm sure you probably take time out to say a real quick blessing at the dinner table, a thank-you-Lord-for-the-food prayer; but how much time do you really take to actually *pray* during each day? As the daily problems arise in your life, do you try to solve them yourself, or do you take time out to send up a real quickie prayer to God?

If you really want to learn to pray and have prayers answered, take time out right now for some real self-evaluation. Do you pray because you have a burden for someone or something? Do you really have a burden for the things of God, or do you take time to pray only when things begin to close in on you?

Before I became a Christian, I knew that God answered prayer, but that was all I knew, and when I really got into a jam, I'd scream, "Oh, God, you do this for me." And then I'd never think about praying again until I got into another jam or mess and really needed help to get me out. I wonder how many times this actually expresses our honest prayer life. And I say honest, because if we are ever going to grow as Christians, we have to be honest with ourselves. So ask yourself, Do I pray only when I'm in a jam, or are my prayers just words that I pray all the time, or are they honest burdens on my heart? Am I genuinely concerned about my fellow man? Or am I just saying words I've said so many times that they don't mean a single thing.

In my various travels there are times when I'm privileged to spend a great deal of time in certain areas or in certain homes. I often discover that by the time I leave I can say their prayers the same as they can, because they never vary them. I've heard, "Thank you, Lord for the blessings you bestow upon our family" and haven't even heard the first blessing they're talking about.

One time I questioned someone on this and said,

"Tell me what you mean by the blessings God bestows on your family."

The answer came back, "Oh, you know, just blessings. I can't really put them into words." You can't? Well, it seems to me that people have no trouble putting everything else into words, so why not to God? You know why? Because you really don't know what you're talking about, and because you really haven't prayed and asked God for specific blessings. So how can you share what he's done?

The prayers I like to hear from people are the ones prayed in thanksgiving, such as, "Lord, how can I thank you enough for sending that car along yesterday with a five gallon can of gas when I had just run out of gas. Somehow you're always there when we need you, so thank you Lord for letting that man come by at just the right time because you knew I had to get to that church meeting on time!" I know that person prayed for something specific, and I know that God really answered that specific prayer.

Come with me on an exciting prayer voyage as I share how God has answered prayers in my life. As we go along I'll share with you some of the reasons why God answers prayer.

# CHAPTER 2

# PRAY BIG

*If you say to this mountain, 'Be taken up
and cast into the sea,' it will be done.*
—Matthew 21:21

MY LIFE is so full of answers to prayer, it's always hard
to know which answers to share in a limited time, or a
limited space. But one of the most thrilling to me and
one of the most powerful, I want to share with you now.

If you have read the story of how I became a Christian, you know that I lost the sight of one eye due to an
automobile accident, the blow loosening the lens of my
eye which then grew back with a cataract. The ophthalmologist told me at the time that probably within a year
I would lose the sight of the other eye. When the second
operation was imminent, I was told I would have a totally blind period for several months. By the time this
occurred, I had found Christ in a most exciting way.

As a result, I resolved to spend the time, when nei-
ther eye would be functioning and I would be bed-
bound, by listening to tapes of sermons or Bible lessons
or even the New Testament. I even fancied memorizing
the entire New Testament while I was waiting for my
eyes to return to a point where contact lens could be
used along with my glasses to allow me to see again.

How the Lord took care of this problem in my life is
what I wanted to write for this chapter, and as I started,
I remembered a letter I had written to my pastor con-

cerning what actually happened. Even though the date of the letter is more than three years old as of this writing, it probably tells the story better than I could retell it today. So if you'd like, I'm going to just quote parts of the letter which came directly from my heart, and it explains why I wrote the letter instead of telling the story firsthand. The only additions I have made are the things I felt were necessary so you would understand the complete meaning of the letter.

June 6, 1966
(really June 7, because it's 2 A.M.)

Dear Rev. Slagle:

I just finished cutting the stencils for your sermon, "It Is Leaven," which will be included with the church news tomorrow. While I was typing it, I had to write you exactly what happened the night I heard this sermon (May 15, 1966).

You remember in February I went to the ophthalmologist because I realized I was having a problem with my right eye, and I heard him say what almost sounded to me like a death sentence—that I was going to lose the sight of my other eye. Even though I came through the first operation successfully, as you well know, it was an extremely difficult time for me, and I certainly didn't relish having to go through it a second time. Especially since I was told there would be a period of time, possibly two months or more, when I would be unable to use either eye.

As I drove from his office to your house, I debated whether to ask God to heal my eye, or whether to commit the situation to him wholly and abide by whatever his wishes were. By the time I got to your house, I had decided to commit the entire problem to God with no selfish request of my own (although I probably cheated a little bit because I reminded him that this would hinder my work in the "GO" program), and I asked you to get some tapes for me to listen to while I was in the hospital and confined at home since I couldn't see to read.

As the weeks went by and my sight became worse, I told you I didn't think I would be able to drive much longer because I couldn't see well in the daylight hours, and absolutely nothing at night! By May 15 I was beginning to feel like a nervous wreck. It was such a problem to drive to Sunday school that morning because I couldn't get anything in focus with either eye (or was it a solution?). I couldn't even read the lesson, nor could I read the words on the pages of the song book that morning in church, so it was a good thing you sang songs I know "by heart."

I often wonder how I got to church that night, my sight was so poor. I prayed as I picked up those I bring to church and asked God to please see that I got them there safely.

And then you preached on "It Is Leaven." I really felt you had a hammer and were personally delivering a real hard wallop on my head with every sentence, and long before you finished I knew I was going to go to the altar and pray that God would heal my eye. No longer did I want to just commit it to him, I wanted to ask him to please touch my eye.

And then came your altar call, and as I took the first step to go, Janice Doe stepped out to accept Christ as her personal Lord and Savior. I stepped back, because I could not detract from her Shining Hour. I would wait for the second altar call.

You made the second altar call, and as I stepped out that first step, I heard the rustle that means someone has answered a call. I stepped back again because I saw that Esther F. had made her decision, and I could not detract from *her* Shining Hour. I would wait for the third altar call.

But you didn't make a third altar call that night, and when I realized that you were not going to make the third call, I almost panicked because I didn't know what to do, so I closed my eyes as the last verse was sung, and said, "Dear God, you know what a lousy prayer I am, so don't listen to HOW I pray, but please, please dear God since you apparently didn't want me to go to the altar tonight, will you reach down and heal my eye?" I also reminded him that I can never remember at crucial moments like this the proper order of things in prayer, like worship, adoration, supplication, etc. I told him I was sure he knows what a complete blank I draw at times like this, but I told him I hoped he knew what was in my heart, even though my head was blank.

I'll never know how I got home that night. Joan (my daughter) gave me directions, but I couldn't even tell where I was and I was so concerned for the lives which were in the car with me. However, you will remember I called you that night and told you that by the time I reached Suniland I could see better than I had for days, even though I knew my eye had not been touched.

All week long I asked God if he wanted me to continue praying that same request, or would that indicate a lack of faith on my part. Was once enough, I wondered, or should I ask again and again and again? I really didn't know what to do, so I read everything I could find in the Bible, knowing somehow that God would send me an answer. During this week, there were two separate occasions when I felt God's hand close, but not close enough to touch my eye.

On Saturday morning, May 21 (and as I write this I realize for the first time that this was the date my other eye had been operated on just one year ago) I went to the beauty parlor as I do every week, and took along the *Living Letters* to read while my hair dried.

The *Living Letters* opened that morning to Ephesians 6:18. If you don't know offhand what it says, you can guess. It says: "Pray all the time. Ask God for anything in line with the Holy Spirit's wishes. Plead with him, reminding him of your needs." I closed that book and, under a dryer in a beauty parlor told God if he wanted me to plead with him, reminding him of my needs, then I was pleading with my heart and my soul to heal this eye. Never have I pleaded as hard as I did this morning, and never have I prayed so fervently I don't believe. And sometime between 8:30 and 8:45, *I saw the hand of God come down and touch my eye.* Now I don't really know how I could have seen it, because I had my eyes closed and before I ever opened my eyes again I said, "Thank you, God," because I knew I didn't have to open my eyes to know what had happened.

And I wondered if you had been praying for me, too. I wanted to fly by and tell you what had happened, because in some of the words of your sermon, you triggered whatever was necessary for my pleading with God.

I know *what* happened, but I'll never know *why,* but who am I to ever question God? But the thing that I think is so fantastic is that God knew exactly who was pleading with him, and knew exactly what beauty parlor he'd find me in, and what dryer he'd find me under. The very same God who hangs out all those stars that I look at through my window at night when I pray in my bedroom before I go to sleep, took time out from the big job he has of watching over the entire universe, to show his love for me.

How could *anyone* doubt there is a God? And how could people not want his Son in their hearts?

I feel better having said this and it comes to you exactly as I felt compelled to write it, with no revisions, no nothing, except a grateful heart.

*Frances*

I never will forget how one time a minister said to me, "You don't believe in that *stuff* like divine healing, do you?"

I very simply answered, "I only believe what the Bible says." And the Bible says if we will ask in the name of Jesus of Nazareth, it shall be done. With my heart and soul I believe that Christ performs as many miracles today as he did two thousand years ago. We are probably more reluctant to talk about them, more reluctant to ask for them and this, I believe, is the reason for the problem. The power of God has not lessened one iota—it's there, and available for those who will believe!

If you're wondering what was in the sermon I mentioned in this chapter, probably the things that hit me were the following sentences: "You have not, because you ask not. You ask for little things, and you get little things; if you want *big* things, ask God for *big* things; if you want God to move a mountain, ask him to move a mountain." God's Holy Spirit had spoken to me through those few words and so because of this, I learned to pray "Big."

# CHAPTER 3

# ASK TO PRAY

*He was praying in a certain place, and
when he ceased, one of his disciples said
to him, "Lord, teach us to pray."*
—Luke 11:1

I SHALL be eternally grateful to Rosalind Rinker for her
inspiring book, *Prayer—Conversing with God!,* because
this book really revolutionized my prayer life. In fact it
*started* my prayer life. I had always thought of prayer as
some formalized collection of words which I didn't really understand (when I listened to a lot of people pray),
and it had a lot of Shakespearean terms such as *thee,
thou,* and *wilt.* This really wilted me because I don't
talk in those terms, and consequently I don't understand
in those terms, either. So I read this book which I believe all new Christians should read, for it makes praying really easy. And the kind of praying I mean is the
"out loud" kind where you can be heard, not only by
God, but by others who want to pray with you.

I think the Lord made my Christian road easy for me
in many respects, because he gave me a burden for
souls. And almost from the start of my Christian life I
have been really blessed because he has used me as a
soul winner. But this can also create a problem, or fur-
nish the answer, whichever way you want to look at it.
Most people look to the person who is their spiritual

"parent" as someone they ask for help in their Christian life. So before I knew it, I was involved in all sorts of requests for prayer, therefore I was really "forced" to learn how to pray.

If you have read or heard the story of how I became a Christian, you know I spent many hours in the bathtub learning to pray. (And I still think it's an excellent place to get clean inside and out!) Because the Lord has placed me in so many exciting situations since I have become a Christian I have really had to learn how to pray for many different reasons. I'd like to share with you how I often teach people to pray.

First of all, there are many different kinds of prayer. There are prayers said from the pulpit, which, of necessity, involve an entire church. Then there are prayers which involve prayer groups which pray for specific needs in a church or in the lives of individuals. But I think the easiest way to learn to pray is just plain talking to God. I'd like to relate to you how I used this little plan to start someone on an exciting prayer life.

In West Virginia I met a couple whose Christian status was quite different from most I have met. The man had been a Christian for many years, while his wife had been a Christian for just a few months. The great bond of Christian love was there immediately and before I had been with this couple ten minutes, the wife said "I want to learn *how* to pray!" And then God laid upon me the burden of teaching her how to pray.

She had offered to drive me to my speaking engagements while I was in West Virginia, so I had the opportunity of sharing with her how I felt about prayer, the need for prayer, the privilege of prayer, the power of prayer, and the constant urge I have for prayer at all times. It's always exciting to see a new Christian with an unquenchable thirst for the things of God, but it seems that prayer is one of the things that really stumps many. Well, nearly everywhere that woman drove me, our conversation centered around prayer.

Then one day as we were driving, I sensed the nudging of the Holy Spirit. I said to her, "Eloise, the Bible says to 'watch and pray' so while you're watching the cars on the freeway, just say, 'Thank you, Lord'. And if you can't get that much out, just say, 'Thank you!' And if you can't get that much out, just say 'Thanks!' "

There was a moment of silence, and then she said, "Okay—I'll do that."

I waited, and nothing happened, so I said, "Okay go ahead!"

Another moment of silence (and do you know how l-o-n-g a moment of complete silence can be?), and then she said, "Right now?"

I said, "Yes, ma'am. Right now!"

Another long pause. "With you in the car?"

I said, "With me in the car." I explained to her that the most difficult "out loud" prayer words you ever say will be the first ones you actually say audibly because the biggest stumbling block of all is opening your mouth that very first time. I said, "There are only the two of us in the car, and in case you're worried that anyone else will think you're crazy talking to yourself, they can see me, and they will think you're talking to me."

I really don't know how far we drove with the conversation repeating itself, but all of a sudden I saw a flush come on her face and she said in a very emotional voice, "Thank you, Lord!" I had been doing my instant praying and my heart really jumped for joy and I said, "God, did you hear that? She actually prayed out loud!" You know, this was an *exciting* thing for her, too. We talked all the rest of the way to our destination as I shared with her how I pray exactly what is on my heart. God doesn't expect us to be geniuses and remember all the mechanics of praying. He only wants to know that we have a sincere heart.

When we returned to the parsonage where I was staying, the pastor's wife brought out a beautiful cake someone had brought over, and asked us to have some. We said we would, and when we sat down, I said, "Eloise, you did so well in the car today, I'm going to ask you to say the blessing now."

Poor Eloise looked as though she wished lightning would strike either her or me, and I think she would have preferred it to have struck me, and she really wilted and said in a completely horrified voice, "In front of the pastor's wife?"

And I said, "In front of the pastor's wife!"

She said, "Oh, *no!*"

And I said, "Oh, *yes!*"

The exciting thing is when you're dealing with someone who is really desirous of growing in Christ, they will do anything because of the Holy Spirit working in their life. And even though she almost emotionally fell apart, Eloise said, "Thank you, Lord, for this cake!" I knew the angels in heaven must have been rejoicing with the Lord to see such eagerness and excitement from someone so willing to learn how to pray.

The next day as I was getting ready to go downtown to be on a radio program, Eloise called to say she would like to drive me down. She said some other women who wanted to learn how to pray would be there too and would like to take me to lunch. Of course I said, "Great!"

At lunch I said, "There's no time like the present to learn to pray. We'll let everyone say either one little word, one little phrase, or one little sentence as a blessing for the food."

And do you know what happened? Eloise blurted out, "I'll pray first, because I've learned how!" My heart really almost banged out of its wall as I realized what an excellent student I had. And, by the way, everyone there got into the prayer act. It's wonderful when several persons accept Christ at the same time because then they can have the fun of growing in grace together. Many individuals have learned to pray around my dinner table because each one was allowed (or forced) to say one sentence, and it's amazing how easy it is to get into the swing of praying, if you will just practice praying, because in prayer, like anything else, practice makes perfect. True, I still haven't discovered what the perfect prayer is like. I don't know what God calls a perfect prayer; I only know he hears mine and answers them in his perfect way.

Some young people I know, who give much of their time to prayer and are some of the most exciting Christians I know, learned to pray around my dinner table in a most unorthodox way. While young people really have an adventuresome spirit for the most part, the idea of praying out loud is a hard thing for a new Christian to do. So before we would actually start the prayer circle around the table, I would ask each one to select the one thing he or she wanted to pray about. Usually about five of them spoke up at one time and the conversation sounded like this: "Dibbies on praying for the pastor." "Dibbies on praying for tonight's service." "Dibbies on praying for the youth meeting next weekend!"

And it was interesting to see how the Holy Spirit guided them into asking for the thing they wanted most to pray for. When you're beginning to learn to pray aloud, it will make your prayer road so much easier and quicker to travel if you will select the things you sincerely want to pray about. Don't think I'm confining anyone to just praying simple little things he wants to pray, but remember the new Christian needs milk and not steak to chew on in the beginning.

I probably will be considered a rebel by many because I also don't feel it's essential to be on your physical knees when praying. You'd better believe I'm on my spiritual knees, but the bulk of my praying is not on my physical knees. Please don't misunderstand me—I have knelt at the altars in many churches, and had such exciting talks with God, and there's something about an altar that really does something for me. But God has answered as many of my prayers when I've been standing, or lying in bed, or driving my car, as any other time. The God who loves me hears my prayers so long as they come from my heart.

Wherever you are right now, just lay down this book for a minute, will you, and say out loud, "Thank you, Lord." If you'd prefer to be where no one can hear you the first time (and that's the way I wanted it), go take a ride in your car, take a walk, jump in the bath tub, or go anyplace where you will have privacy, but say *out loud* those three little words.

Are you back now? Did it almost choke you the first time? But believe me, if you really mean business, the next time won't be nearly as bad. And before you know it, it will become one of the most exciting things in your life. Now you're ready for the second step.

You've said "Thank you, Lord," but you didn't really say what for, did you? Okay, just think of one little thing the Lord has done for you. If you can't think of anything, let me help you a little bit. Did he die on a cross for you and me? Could you thank him for that? (I mean *out loud!*) All right, let's try it. You think that's too hard? Well, let's see, how's the weather where you are? Could you thank him for the kind of day it is? And you know, we should really thank him whatever the day is because some exciting thing will come of it, regardless of what the weather is like. Or could you thank him for giving you enough to eat? Or could you thank him for a good night's rest? Or could you thank him for the privilege of being alive? Or could you thank him for the privilege he's given you of knowing how to read a book?

Well, if you don't have a case of emotional jitters by

now, you're ready for the next step. If I were your best friend and you were having a problem, say, with your husband, you would probably confide in me and tell me what your husband had been doing to make your marriage unhappy (or what your wife had been doing to make your marriage unhappy if you're the husband). So you'd probably say something like this: "You know, Joe drives me out of my mind. I work so hard trying to keep this house clean and every night when he comes home, it's the same thing.

"He leaves his shoes for me to fall over or pick up. And every morning I find he's left the top off the toothpaste. He knows how irritated this makes me, but he does it all the time. Then when I ask him to take out the garbage, or wash the dishes, he says, 'What do you think I am? That's a woman's work, not a man's work!' You know I just go through this day after day until I'm absolutely a nervous wreck."

Now the funny thing is we can tell all these little faults about our husbands to our friends, and it gets us nowhere, but would you really like to know a much better solution? You would? Well, you've probably guessed it by now—just get on that *Hot Line to Heaven* and use it.

Your conversation with God might sound something like this: "Good morning, God, here I am again. You know, I've got a real problem and I'd like you to show me how to handle it. You know I can't get my Sunday school lesson studied because every day it's the same old thing. I clean this house over and over and then when Joe comes home, he leaves his shoes in the living room, and I have to keep picking them up. And Lord, you know how it aggravates me when he leaves the top off the toothpaste, and when I fight with him over the garbage I get so upset I could just die. Lord, please either straighten Joe out, or teach me to have more patience, love, and understanding."

You know, if you really prayed like that, you'd have peace flood your soul, because instead of just imbedding a situation into your mind, you would have really done something constructive about it. You would have asked for God's guidance. Now don't laugh, if God knows how many hairs are on your head, don't you think he cares about everything where you're concerned?

And don't you think he's glad you give him the opportunity of helping you? You know Christ will never force himself upon you, but he patiently waits for you to ask. You see, whether we daily take advantage of the power of prayer or not, Christ patiently waits for the first word from us, so it's never a question of no one answering when we use that *Hot Line to Heaven.* You never get the busy signal, because God is never too busy. He waits to hear what you have to say and wants to answer your prayers.

If you're a husband with a miserable wife (and you know *no* woman is a miserable wife, don't you?) you can make up your own imaginary conversation about her sloppy habits, and then visualize and verbalize what you would say to God about the same situation. And then, most important of all, *listen* to what God has to say to you.

That last sentence has a lot in it. Do you realize that one of the most important things in prayer is waiting to hear what God has to say to you? So many times we impatiently pray and then, because we don't feel that God at *that* moment is going to do anything about it, we take our little problem back and try to solve it all by ourselves. As a matter of fact, so many times we are so busy asking everyone's advice about our problems, that we aren't still long enough to discover what God has to say to us. Remember what I said at the beginning of the book about *giving* your prayer request to God, and then turning your hand over and dropping your arm down to your side. So part of the secret of prayer, then, is to take time to listen to God's answers.

As a normal rule I don't tell people to ask God to "tell" them something, because some expect a loud booming voice to come out of the woodwork or some other place, giving them explicit instructions. God *will* give you explicit instructions, but you must know how to recognize his answers. I would suggest that you ask God to *reveal* to you what he wants you to do in a certain situation. Many times the answer will come to us through another person. God sometimes uses others to convey to us what he wants from our life. God's Word is so helpful for answers to prayer, and often the Lord of my life will lead me to a scripture which answers my prayer just as though he had written a personal letter to me. Many times through a series of situations, God will reveal his plan for you, or the answer to your prayer.

I do hope you'll remember one thing, though. God doesn't always answer our prayers as we think they ought to be answered. Why? God is a lot smarter than any of us, and I've learned to accept his answers, knowing that whatever he has planned for me is far better than anything I could ever hope to plan myself. So even if you get an answer that seems not quite what you want, trust God for the needs of your life, and you'll be amazed how much better your life turns out to be.

# CHAPTER 4

# PRAY FOR WISDOM

*If any of you lacks wisdom, let him ask God, who gives to all men generously and without reproaching, and it will be given him. But let him ask in faith, with no doubting, for he who doubts is like a wave of the sea that is driven and tossed by the wind.*
　　　　　　　　　　　　—James 1:5-6

THE ABOVE scripture is one which more people ought to remember and use. In my own life, it became real when God laid the burden on me to write the story of how I became a Christian.

I was not fortunate enough to attend college, and so I have only a high school education, and had never written a single article in my life, not even a column for the high school paper. At the age of fifty I realized it's hard to "teach an old dog new tricks." But new tricks I did learn—to be more specific, I asked for wisdom, in faith believing, and here's the way it happened.

I believe one of the strongest burdens the Lord has ever laid upon me was to write the story of my life. I couldn't understand it at all, because I felt how I became a Christian was probably a lot like everyone else, but I constantly had the nagging, gnawing feeling that I *had* to write the story of how I became a Christian. Because I'm always eager to obey God and do whatever he calls me to do, I sat down at my typewriter after work one night and started to write the story of how I found Christ.

Night after night I would do the same thing. I would wait until everyone left the office, then I would roll a sheet of paper into the typewriter and start out, "I became a Christian at the ripe old age of forty-nine." And then my inspiration would completely stop. I would begin another sentence with "At the age of forty-nine I became a Christian." Then I would decide that wasn't such a good start, insert another sheet and type "Forty-nine was my age when I became a Christian." Then I would be stuck again. I would make another stab at it. I would write a few sentences and then say to myself, "That really stinks!" And then I'd remind God that I wasn't a writer, and that I never would be a writer. But God's Holy Spirit was completely relentless with me (as he always is, PTL*). I knew that I would never rest until I had done what God wanted me to do, and yet I felt so completely inadequate for the task.

I was talking on the phone to a pastor one night, and told him that God had really laid on me such a burden to write the story of my life, and yet I just couldn't seem to do it. He gave me some of the greatest words of advice anyone has ever given to me. He said, "Frances, go back to your typewriter and pray, and give God your fingers and your brains and ask him to use them to write the story he wants written."

I hung up and went over to my typewriter and prayed, just a very simple, short prayer. I held out my hands and said, "Lord, these are my fingers." Pointing to my head I said, "And this is my brain. They're yours. Let your Holy Spirit use them to write the story you want written."

I put a piece of paper into my typewriter, and my

*Praise the Lord. The initialed expression was popularized by members of the Fellowship of Christian Athletics.

fingers flew. The words just came out so fast I could hardly keep up with them (and I happen to be an unusually fast typist). Thirty hours after I started, the book, my first, *God Is Fabulous,* was completed. I never rewrote it; I never edited it; and my publisher changed only a few words in it. And I've never been able to take any credit for it, either. With my heart and soul I believe that God's Holy Spirit directed the writing of it, and when the inspiration ended, it ended. There was no more to that particular book. Prayer had done it again! I had asked for wisdom and knowledge to write a book, and God, hearing my simple prayer, had immediately answered.

Before long, another urge welled up in me, and that was to write a book in which I would share how easy it is to tell the simple story of Jesus Christ to everybody. Again I prayed for wisdom, and again my fingers and my brain were given to the Lord as I prayed to be nothing but an open channel through which his Holy Spirit could work. Again another book flew out of my finger tips. I never rewrote this one, or edited it, and the completed manuscript was soon published. But, again, I feel the credit belongs to someone else, not to me.

And then my pastor's wife was talking one day to someone who made the comment, "Frances must have a hot line to heaven because God answers so many of her prayers." And with this little tidbit came the inspiration for this third book. Again, as I prayed for wisdom and guidance, giving my fingers and brains to the Lord, the story you are reading welled up within me and I felt it would just run all over the place if I didn't put it on paper. I have been unable to contain myself as the chapters of this book unfold.

The things that I'm sharing with you are intimate things which personally concern me, and yet as I write them I'm fascinated with how they are brought to my mind. One comment I would like to make about this book, though, is the fact that the devil trembles where prayer is concerned because he knows the power of prayer. And because this book deals with prayer, he has thrown every roadblock in the way you could possibly imagine to keep me from completing it on schedule. My office has been too busy, personnel problems have bogged us down, causing me to work night after night until early morning just to keep the office going, without any quiet time to put on paper the thoughts I have concerning prayer.

Never have I ever seen the devil so determined to stop anything as he has been to stop this book. Never have I prayed so much over any book, and never have I ever realized the strength and power of the devil as I have where this book is concerned. Finally, in complete helplessness, I cried out to God through the power of his Holy Spirit to bind the hands of satan and allow me to finish the book on schedule. God heard my cry and even though the devil fought every inch of the way he went down to defeat.

As I think of the title of this book, *Hot Line to Heaven,* I can't help but think how true that statement really is. I have often said, "God is as close as your telephone." We all have a private or "hot line" to heaven, but the only problem we have is that we don't all use it the same. Right now I'm looking at my telephone on my desk. What a marvelous little instrument it is. I have only to pick it up, push some little buttons correctly, and within a matter of seconds I can be talking to someone in California, or Honolulu, or any place in the whole world. But as long as that little instrument sits there and I don't pick it up, it isn't going to be worth very much in my life, is it?

The same thing is true of prayer, our hot line to heaven. There it is, a direct line, no other parties on the same line you're on, so you never get the busy signal when you dial GOD. But how often do you really dial him? How often do you call upon him to answer even your smallest needs.

I have learned from personal experience that I can stand upon the promises of the Bible and let my entire life be guided by a hot line to heaven. I used to wonder if God got tired of my saying "Here I am again, Lord," but he continued to answer my prayers to such a fabulous degree that I finally quit asking him that and just prayed constantly for every single little area in my life.

# CHAPTER 5

## PRAY WITH FLEECES

I AM a great "fleece" thrower. And if you don't know what I'm talking about, I'd like to quote five long, but very interesting, verses from the Old Testament. Judges 6:36-40. If you don't know the story, let me share with you my understanding of this Bible story.

God had called Gideon to deliver Israel, but Gideon was afraid, so he asked God to give him an answer so there could be no doubt in his mind. Read these verses right now with this in mind: "Then Gideon said to God, If thou wilt deliver Israel by my hand, as thou hast said, behold, I am laying a fleece of wool on the threshing floor; if there is dew on the fleece alone, and it is dry on all the ground, then I shall know that thou wilt deliver Israel by my hand, as thou hast said. And *it was so.* When he rose early next morning and squeezed the fleece, he wrung enough dew from the fleece to fill a bowl of water. Then Gideon said to God, 'Let not thy anger burn against me, let me speak but this once; pray, let me make trial only this once with the fleece; pray, let it be dry only on the fleece, and on all the ground let there be dew.' And *God did so that night;* for it was dry on the fleece only, and on all the ground there was dew."

You see, Gideon so doubted what God had told him, that he asked for visible proof of God's will for his life. Was it really doubting, or did Gideon want absolute and positive direction? I honestly feel he wanted positive direction, because in my own life there have been times when I could not clearly understand what God wanted for my life, and so that there could be no doubt, I have thrown out a fleece. If you carefully read Gideon's prayers, you will note that God answered both times, even though the second request was exactly the opposite of the first.

I remember the first fleece I ever threw out. After my first book was published, I received many invitations to speak in churches. I felt that God had placed a special call on my life, and I couldn't exactly figure out what it was. I knew it would be exciting, whatever it was, but I couldn't see how I could still run a business and accept speaking dates. Yet I knew I had to do what God had called me to do. My question: how could I be sure what that was? Then, remembering the story of Gideon, I decided to throw out a fleece.

Here is what I prayed: "Lord, I don't care what you want from my life, all I want to know is definitely and positively what it is you want me to do. If you want me to share the excitement I feel about your son Jesus Christ with all these churches inviting me to visit them, will you (*I was going to make the fleece a really difficult one for him, so I thought*)."

Continuing my prayer, I said, "Will you get me an invitation to speak in the ———— Church" and I selected a very large, well known church. I knew I didn't have a chance in a million to ever be asked to speak there, so I knew that I would be safe and secure in my little printing business. Well, this was on Monday that I prayed, and Tuesday I zoomed through my work; Wednesday nothing happened, Thursday, nothing happened—my mail wasn't flooded with invitations to speak in this particular church, and *then came Friday*. As I was sitting at my desk in the office, the door opened, and in walked the pastor of this particular church. He said, "Frances, we were vacationing in West Palm Beach, and I wanted to call you, but I was afraid you might say no, so we decided instead to drive down so you couldn't tell us no, because *We want to extend an invitation to you to speak in . . .*" and he named the particular church.

I was actually frozen to my chair because I felt as if a bolt of lightning had gone down my soggy spaghetti spine, and you'd better believe that I said yes. God had so powerfully answered my prayer and had picked up the fleece that it left no doubt in my mind what he wanted for me.

One of the most interesting things about this particular invitation is that it has not been consummated to date. But notice how I worded my prayer request. I asked only to receive an *invitation* to speak. I did not ask to speak, and God picked up the fleece *exactly as I had asked;* he saw to it that I received an invitation to speak. This is another reason we should be careful *how* we pray, because God answers prayer!

In conjunction with my business I have thrown out many fleeces. When God first put the call on my life, I thought he wanted me to sell my business and devote myself to full time Christian service. But I've discovered you can be in full time Christian service and still be in business as well. I was so positive he wanted me to sell my business I almost put it up for sale. Then I remembered Gideon, so I threw out the fleece again. But this time it *lay right there*. I couldn't understand it, because

I had felt so positive this was the Lord's will (or was it really mine?) and yet as I look back on it now, I realize the reason behind it. Over the years, I have received many excellent offers for my business, and yet when I threw out the fleece, all offers stopped coming, so I said, "Well, Lord, if that's the way you want it, you must have a reason, so that's all right with me."

Since that time he has revealed to me that my greatest leverage in talking to men is because I'm a businesswoman and can talk to them on their own level. I am not talking to them as someone who doesn't know anything about the business world, but I deal with men every day in a man's competitive world. So I can understand—and shoot holes in—their reasons for not becoming a Christian. And by the way, men, in case you're wondering, I own a printing company, and while we *sell* printing, we *give* Jesus Christ with every order. And I have not yet lost the first customer because of sharing Jesus Christ. A stimulus is my motto, which is "Wherever I go, God goes with me, and that makes me a majority." And as I naturally share Christ, it's amazing what God's power will do even in a business office!

Another very thrilling prayer experience concerns Gene Cotton, recipient of the gooey, whipped cream, cherry pie the Lord delivered via a huge jet. Gene and I became acquainted through Alpha/Omega, a Christian youth movement I founded, and it was exciting how our paths continued to cross. Gene is a most outstanding Christian young man, a very meaningful folk singer. It seemed every time I turned around there was an opportunity for Gene to sing in the Miami area instead of around his home town of Columbus, Ohio. So I would call Gene and he would fly down. While he was in Miami for his singing engagements, we spent many hours around my dining room table having the most exciting prayer circles. The Christian love which abounded around that table was just fabulous! Many times there would be fifteen or twenty of us around the table, listening to the guidance of the Holy Spirit as we learned to pray more and more all the time.

After Gene had made several trips to the Miami area, he was going to New York where I made arrangements for him to audition with one of the larger record companies. As he was leaving his home in Columbus, Ohio, to drive to New York, he called me and after a brief conversation said, "Frances, I wish you'd be my manager."

I said, "What did you say?"

He repeated very simply, "I wish you'd be my manager."

I said, "How could I ever be your manager? I don't know the first thing about singing; I don't know the first thing about music; I don't know the first thing about show business; I don't know the first thing about booking, or anything else."

Gene's answer was very simple, but very profound. He said, "I don't care about that, I only know that when you pray with me, it gives me spiritual strength."

I really didn't know what to say, so I said, "Well, you pray about it, and I'll pray about it, and you call me tomorrow when you get to New York and we'll see." I hung up the telephone that Sunday afternoon and said, "Lord, what would you have me do?" I really began praying earnestly, because had I used "common sense" my answer would have been "Go find yourself a manager who knows something about show business." But God was dealing in the situation, so I just couldn't say no. I examined myself, asking myself many questions that Sunday afternoon. I said, Am I getting so old and senile that I think it would be fun to run around the country after a young folk singer? Then I thought, Or am I afraid of getting old so I want to run after youth? I talked to my pastor, and to another pastor who knew both of us, and they seemed in agreement that God had spoken, but I was still not convinced. I prayed and prayed, and when I fervently pray for an answer, I am actually in anguish until God's answer comes. I never stop praying until I know what God wants me to do. I was still praying five hours later when it was time to go to evening worship.

Arriving a little early, I was sitting alone, holding my beloved Bible. All of a sudden, I threw a fleece. I said, "Lord, you know how dumb I am, because I just don't seem to be able to get your answer, and you know it doesn't make any difference to me what you answer, whether you want me to go to New York, or stay here, or whether you want me to be his manager or not. I only want to make sure that your will is done in this matter. So, Lord, I *know* there is an answer in your Word. Whatever the answer is, reveal it to me in the pages of my Bible. Whatever your answer is, I'll be happy."

With that I opened the Bible, and it was upside down. I turned the Bible up the right way, and two verses came into sharp focus. Before I quote you Romans 1:11-12, I want you to stop and recall the *only* reason Gene gave for wanting me to be his manager, then listen to what God gave me as an answer: "For I long to see you, that I may impart to you some spiritual gift to strengthen you, that is, that we may be mutually encouraged by each other's faith, both yours and mine." God's love so completely enveloped me after I had tortuously searched for his will, that I felt a peace and calm that was indescribable. You might be interested in knowing that I took the next plane to New York.

The prayer angle of this story might have ended right here but it didn't, because one of the most outstanding prayer nights I have ever spent was a result of this whole day of prayer.

I flew to New York with a contract to sign as Gene's manager and Gene and a friend of his met me at the plane. They had made reservations for me at the same hotel where they were staying, and this was an experience from the word "Go." Nestled in the heart of Greenwich Village was this unbelievable hotel. I almost panicked at the thought of staying in a place like this, but since we were close to where the auditions were held, it was the most feasible place to stay. Not only that, Gene and his friend were really short on money, and I didn't want to stay uptown by myself, so decided to "rough it."

With much prayer, in the dingiest hotel room I've ever been in in my entire life, we signed the contract with Star McClendon watching. No contract was really necessary, because we made an agreement with God concerning the kind of career Gene was to have, and one of the covenants was that Gene would never give any kind of performance without at least one Christian song to bear witness to the fact that he was a Christian.

The big audition was the following night, and the three of us prayed all day long about which four songs Gene should sing. After all, an audition with a big record company, and only four songs to show a variety of talent, left us in a quandary. Should it be a fast one, then a slow one? Should Gene play the banjo or not? We finally decided on the four songs, but forgot our covenant with God. On the first opportunity the Lord had provided for us, we selected four secular songs.

We left the hotel early to arrive in plenty of time at the coffee house where the auditions were held. I had never before been in a coffee house and was intrigued because it was so dark. The contact I wear to give me sight in the one eye had gotten a rough edge and irritated my eye. I removed the lens, which resulted in my not seeing too well.

Gene and Star went to where the performers were lining up, and I went to the ladies room to powder my nose. It was so dark—the only light being the gas flame under the huge coffee pot—that I didn't see a big step-down, and I fell flat as a pancake! I fell so hard I really saw stars and remember thinking, "How come I thought it was so dark in here—just look at all those beautiful lights!" And then before I knew it, a whole army of people had come to pick me up off the floor. I very calmly said, "My foot is broken!"

What actually happened was my heel had caught on the edge of the step and violently thrown my foot over the edge! The waiters (or some one) finally got me up and sat me down at a table. I didn't want them to call a doctor, because I felt Gene would get upset if he knew I had fallen, so I sat there until he had finished singing his four songs (without a religious one) and we stayed for a little while longer, then I finally told the guys what had happened and we decided I'd better get to a doctor or something because by this time I was beginning to be in pain.

The rest of the night was a horrible comedy. We took the cab back to the hotel and I tried soaking my foot, first in cold water and then hot. The pain kept getting worse until finally we decided I had better get to a hospital. We were on about the fifth floor in this old run-down hotel, about a block from the elevator. It seems to me there must have been two buildings which were separate at one time, and they joined them by going through the fire wall on each floor, and the part we were in was on the far side from the elevators. To go from one building to the next it was necessary to go single file up two stairs through the opening and then you were in the other building. While some of the "guests" of this hotel were simply "out of this world," I have often wondered since then if we didn't look "Out of this world," too.

By this time the pain was so great I couldn't put any pressure on my foot. So Gene and Star made a seat by grabbing each other's wrists so they could carry me (because I'm too much of a load for any one person to carry). We started down the long hotel corridor, around the bend, up the stairs, then they had to let me go and just let me hang onto the wall, because the narrow opening between the two buildings wasn't big enough for them to carry me through. Even though I could have cried from the pain, we had to laugh at the ridiculous situation. They finally got me down to the lobby (if it could be called that) of the hotel and the night clerk said we'd have to stand on the street and he would call an ambulance.

It seems there had been a subway accident and all the ambulances were at the scene of the accident, so the hospital said they couldn't send one, but suggested we call a taxi. I don't know exactly what time it was, but it was probably around midnight, and we couldn't see a cab anywhere. Star and Gene couldn't go looking for a cab because I couldn't stand on my foot at all. However, finally deciding they would have to go looking for a cab, they draped me around a lamp post on the corner and went in search of a cab. All I could think of was what a picture we must have presented: two young men, one white, one black, and a woman older than their mothers, and I was draped around a lamp post on a street corner in New York with no shoe on my one foot. I'm sure I must have looked like a drunk to anyone who passed by.

A police car stopped, but because I was from out of state, they wouldn't take me in a police car. But they did get a cab. So with the police car leading and the light flashing, we went to a hospital in downtown New York. The police radioed ahead so I was met with a wheel chair, wheeled into the emergency room, and left waiting. Gene and Star were left out in the waiting room. My foot was X-rayed, and while I was waiting for the verdict, I sat there several hours watching the dregs of humanity come through the emergency room door. I saw a woman who had been carved into ribbons by her lover. I saw a dope addict screaming for help. I saw almost every kind of human misery as I sat there through the long night.

Finally I was told that my foot was broken in three places and they were trying to get an orthopedic surgeon to set it, an especially important procedure because of my age. I had almost prayed myself out and then I got to the point where I was in such agony I couldn't even pray any more. I had been given nothing for pain, and even though I have a very high pain tolerance, I felt I had taken about all I could stand. I was figuratively climbing the walls.

Finally at 5 A.M. the nurse told me they were unable to get the orthopedic man, so they put a pressure dressing on my foot, and gave me a pair of crutches. I was advised to go to the City Hospital the next day to have the cast put on my foot. In the meantime I could go back to the hotel. I finally asked if they could give me something for the pain, so they gave me some kind of pill to take, wheeled me down the hall, and deposited me with Gene and Star.

I could take pages telling you how the fellows had to carry me up the stairs to the lobby of the hotel, around to the elevator, and then down the block long corridor before they finally got me back to my room. By this time there were some good arguments going on in the hotel and I decided it was about the last place in the world I wanted to be.

When they finally deposited me in the room, I looked at Gene and said, "The very first night we had a contract and made the covenant with God, what did we do? We blew it! You didn't sing a religious song." I never felt so convicted of sin in my entire life as I did that night. I said, "God, I'm sorry, but I promise you this, as long as I have anything to do with Gene's career, he will never fail to sing a Christian song, regardless of where he is." A verse in Hebrews came to me: "For the Lord disciplines him whom he loves, and chastises every son whom he receives."

I took my Bible to bed. The next day Star and Gene made the rounds of agencies, but I spent the entire time in bed, just talking to God. He knew my contrite heart; he knew the depth of my sorrow at having broken a promise. And God certainly knew I would never do it again. Because I knew what I had done, and because I had "Godly sorrow" I prayed and prayed and prayed, and begged God for his great mercy and love and asked him to heal the breaks in my foot, because I knew what this would do to hinder the work I had to do for him.

Nothing has ever done so much for my spiritual life as this Gethsemane. I did nothing but pray until it was time to go to the hospital in the late afternoon, and yet somehow I knew that God's mighty power had worked in a smelly, dirty hotel room which was about as "unspiritual" a place as I've ever seen.

I managed to get dressed, and as we left to go to the hospital, I said to Gene: "I *know* God has healed my foot!" We went to the hospital, and after going through all kinds of red tape I finally got to a doctor. Then I made the simple statement, "I'm going home, because I want my foot set by a doctor who will be close to me if I run into trouble." So I signed myself out, went back to the hotel, and made a reservation to go home.

We took a cab to the airport, crutches, pressure dressing and all, and it looked for a moment as if we would miss the plane. But Gene finally ran ahead, and I threw caution to the winds, and with my crutches flying, I *ran down the ramp to the airplane,* limping as I went. As I got to the stairs (they were holding the plane for me), I leaned over to kiss Gene and Star goodbye, and Gene very slyly said to me, "You're limping on the *wrong* foot!"

I said, "I know it. I told you that the *right* physician had treated my foot."

My family in Miami had been alerted to the broken foot, so they were at the airport, and Eastern furnished a wheelchair to take me off the plane and into the car. All the while inside of me I *knew* that my foot had been healed. It's a peculiar thing, but when you're new in Christ, you feel like an idiot telling people things like this. I *knew* everyone would think I was a real moron because in the twentieth century God just does not heal any more. On, no?

Well, I played real invalid that night, and the next day I went to work on crutches, but when no one was looking, I walked without them, and then that afternoon I went to my own doctor for X-rays. I didn't have to go, because I already *knew* the answer. *The breaks were no longer there.*

And to be real honest, I said, "Lord, I don't care if people think I'm crazy or not, you've done it again, and I've got to tell them I'm once again whole." I threw the crutches away, but you know what? No one laughed at my story. There I stood with visible proof. I couldn't even have sprained my ankle and two days later thrown away the crutches, let alone have three breaks and not even have one small pain two days later. Not in the normal course of events.

The power of prayer had again been revealed to me! God's love, his grace and his mercy had again been shown to me. There are many people who might wonder why I spend every available moment running around for God. How could I do anything else? How could I ever hope to repay him for all he's done for me? I couldn't.

How could I ever doubt the power of prayer? I couldn't.

On a recent tour I had been on a radio program in a small midwestern town, and as I was leaving the station, the pastor asked me if I would mind seeing a woman of bad reputation. Her name had been given to him by a parole officer. Her criminal record was long. All of her five children had been taken away from her. One of them, a fifteen-year-old girl, was in a home for unwed mothers, expecting her first baby. Two boys were in jail, and the two youngest children were in a home for delinquents. Some church people had decided it would be wonderful if I could "convert" her. I often wonder why people fail to realize that only God can make the increase, certainly none of us.

As always before speaking on radio, I had prayed, asking God to prepare some special person to hear the message he wanted me to share that morning. And then I prayed that he would give me the right words to say. I shared for about thirty minutes of the things of God that I find so magnificent. Leaving the station, I prayed again, this time for the woman I had been asked to see. Sometimes people expect so much, but this is one of the things that makes me so totally dependent upon God, because I realize *I can't do it*. I really sent up a storm of prayer asking God to use me in dealing with this woman's eternal destiny.

We knocked on her door, I introduced myself, and she looked at me absolutely stunned. She stammered, "Are—are you the one who was just on the radio?" and pointed to a radio high on a kitchen shelf. I nodded yes and then she said an amazing thing: "I started to turn that program off because I don't listen to that religious stuff. But when I put my hand up to turn the dial, my hand froze right in mid air. I had to listen to what you were saying, and when you finished, I said to that radio: 'I wish I could meet someone like that!' And here you are. I just don't believe it." How quickly God had begun to work in her life!

She asked us to sit down. I had to move ashtrays full of cigaret and cigar butts and push away several glasses which contained the remnants of drinks. I placed my precious Bible down on the table. I prayed that God would really undergird me, and I believe that for every word I said to her I must have prayed about twenty to God, for I really needed help in this situation.

God's Holy Spirit really enveloped that dirty, filthy room and after I had read the four spiritual laws to the woman, I asked her if there was any reason she wouldn't like to receive Christ *right now*. She said "No, there isn't any reason at all." The three of us prayed right there with heads bowed. When I looked up at the end of the prayer, God had transformed someone right in front of my eyes.

The woman who had bowed her head as a sinner was not the same woman I saw just a few minutes later. Everything about her seemed different and she smiled a beautiful smile and said, "You know what? I like you folks!" What she was really saying was that she had seen God's love through two human beings. And then she said, "I believe God's going to give me back my children!" I was thrilled to see such a radical change in her so quickly. Even her features looked so much softer than they had previously.

Prayer had been the forerunner—and prayer had done the work even before I knew who was the target of God's message that day.

# CHAPTER 6

# PRAY CONSTANTLY

*Rejoice always, pray constantly, give
thanks in all circumstances; for this is the
will of God in Christ Jesus for you.*
— 1 Thessalonians 5:16-17

How I pray that I may communicate to every single
reader the importance of praying *constantly*. I wish I
knew exactly how I learned to pray all the time. Even
when I'm working in the office, or talking to a person,
or talking on the telephone, or doing any of the tasks I
have to perform during a day, I am in constant conversation with God. Perhaps there's the ability to divide
yourself in half, and do what God says: work *and* pray.

When I first learned to pray, I felt that prayer had to
be at certain times only. But as I grew and Christ became more real in my life, I learned to depend more
and more on him. Perhaps the reason God has given me
this faith is the fact that I probably tested him just a tiny
little bit in the beginning. And he answered my prayer.
And then I asked for a little bigger request. And he answered that prayer. And then I asked for a little bigger
request. And he again answered my prayer. Like climbing a ladder a step at a time, I learned how to pray constantly. I pray constantly when I'm driving the car, or
wherever I am. God gives us the ability to stay in constant fellowship with him.

Probably the reason I see so many exciting prayer answers is because I pray constantly, knowing and believing that God will answer in an exciting way!

On one of my speaking trips, I had to fly on a very small airplane over mountainous country. It had been years since I had been in such a small craft, so when I got on I said to the attendant, "Do you pass out goggles and helmets?" That's what I felt I needed, although, honestly, it wasn't an open cockpit plane.

However, when these smaller planes fly low over the mountains and get caught in the turbulence, they are really rough to ride. I got greener and greener—and here I was on my way to a speaking engagement. The greener I got, the sicker I felt.

The stewardess kept asking if I felt all right, and I kept insisting I was fine. But I really knew that things were happening that shouldn't be happening.

I was so concerned with the sudden way the plane dipped and bobbed, I prayed that the Lord would see to it we got safely to our destination. We did, but when I got off, I'm sure I was the greenest speaker that pastor had ever met. Did you ever try to feel dignified and "spiritual" when you *knew* you were going to throw up? Don't try—it's impossible.

As I staggered off the plane and was met by the pastor of my host church, my first words were, "You'd better pray that I don't get sick, *right now!*" And because he was the kind of minister who saw that I really meant it, he didn't cross me off as a real nut. He held my hands and we prayed standing there at the airport that God's healing touch would be on my sick stomach and grant me peace. Like a stream of cool water, the power of God became evident, and the power of prayer became known, because as I was bathed in answered prayer, all signs of stomach sickness left me.

Do I believe this was coincidence? No, I do not. I *know* beyond a shadow of doubt it was an immediate answer to prayer. Before I became a Christian, I had gotten airsick many times, and in great determination I would make up my mind I wasn't going to get sick. But in spite of all my determination I've been in bed for two days afterward trying to get over motion sickness so I know this was not a coincidence in any way. God loves for us to put our requests before him, because he loves us so much he wants to answer them.

A little while later, as I left this town to come out of the mountains, I had to fly the same line. This time before I got on I prayed that the Lord would keep my stomach from feeling so queasy. And sure enough I maintained my equilibrium and didn't get sick at all, *but* . . . my ears plugged up. And as anyone who has ear problems in the air knows, this can really hurt and be uncomfortable. I wouldn't have minded at all, except I knew I was scheduled to be on a TV program, and when my ears are plugged up, it definitely affects my voice.

Well, I held my ears; I blew my nose; I chewed about ten pieces of gum—I sat on a chair and hung my head over the side. I tried all the suggested remedies as I was getting dressed to go to the TV station, and then I suddenly realized what a nut I was. All God wanted me to do was to ask him to alleviate the problem, so I just quickly prayed and said "Lord I'm really a nut because I know all I have to do is to ask and I will receive. I don't really understand how you do it, Lord, I only know and believe that you can and will, so please, Lord, would you unplug my ears?" I'm sure I don't have to tell you what happened, do I? Because you know the answer. Again—coincidence? *No,* only answered prayer.

In my house we pray constantly for all kinds of exciting things—and also dull things, depending on how you want to look at it. If there isn't an urgent need at the moment, we just thank God for some of the fabulous things he's done for us. And sometimes, just because it's like a dip in a cool mountain stream on a hot day, we just say, "Praise the Lord." Even as I teach my Sunday school class I'm led to have someone say "Praise the Lord," because no one can scowl and say "Praise the Lord." Sometimes our prayers should be just to praise the Lord for his goodness to us.

One night while we were eating dinner, my daughter said, "Mother, I really need some money in a hurry, because I haven't had any baby sitting jobs recently. I won't have any money to give to God Sunday if I don't get a job before this week is out."

I said, "Well, honey, let's just pray *right now* and ask God to see that you get a baby sitting job before the weekend so you can have your money for church." We stopped right in the middle of our dinner (we pray just any old time) and asked God to nudge someone needing a babysitter and remind them of Joan's capability. We thanked God for answering prayer and couldn't wait to see who would call. Before the meal was finished, the telephone rang, and—you're right—it was a family calling for Joan to baby-sit over the weekend.

As I stated previously in this book, our comment many times is, "So soon, Lord?" But you see, God knows when a need is desperate and when the prayer needs to be answered *right now*.

I hope, in the requests listed in this chapter on the "praying constantly" kind of prayer, you will notice the underlying reason in each case. In each case the request is made in order that we might serve God in a pleasing manner.

I'm reminded of a home I had been invited to in one of the cities I visited, and I didn't know why I had been invited until after I arrived. A group of people present, obviously searching, had been brought there by the hostess for me to share what Christ had done in my life. My own personal testimony is a story I see repeated over and over again in every city I visit. People have sat in church all their life and are virtual prisoners of religion, but many don't know Christ at all or the freedom he brings.

It wasn't long before I realized which one the Lord had called me to minister to: a very lovely woman, talented, faithful in her churchgoing, but without personal relationship to Christ. I immediately began praying because I knew this was going to be a difficult situation. She was very haughty and was determined to knife me into little ribbons (so she thought). But she didn't know that God with me makes a majority.

She very nastily said to me, "Are you saying you don't think I'm a Christian?" Realizing how necessary it is to pray for God's grace while talking to an individual like this, I was bombarding the gates of heaven, asking that God's Holy Spirit reveal to me the correct answers. I asked Christ to let his love shine through me to reach this woman who so needed to know Christ in a personal way.

She asked me all kinds of questions and I had to continue to ask for guidance and knowledge in this instance. I could sense her hostility and, oh, how I prayed that God's love would break through her barriers, and I prayed constantly that my natural instincts, or self, or ego, or whatever you want to call it, would not come through with a desire to verbally "lay her out" for being so cutting and cruel.

God's Holy Spirit so enveloped me that no evil could harm me, and my constant storming heaven's gates for almost three hours brought a most amazing ending to the evening. As we stood to leave, I suggested we form a prayer circle and pray. Now by a prayer circle I mean a holding of hands, because I firmly believe God's power can electrify a room. From one strong Christian warrior this power can pass through and strengthen some weak ones in the circle. There is something about contact in prayer that does something to a group.

I always pray as I feel led by the Holy Spirit, and

while it might upon occasion go right around the room in a circle, most of the time it will go from one to another without any particular order or sequence. We started praying, and all of a sudden we heard the voice of the woman with the rebellion, and she said, "If false pride is keeping me from becoming a Christian, forgive me. I don't *know* if I'm a Christian or not. Christ, I want to invite you into my life right now. I ask you to forgive my sins, but most of all to forgive the sins I have committed this night to someone who was trying to show me your love." I don't believe there was a dry eye in the house. Naturally, I didn't have to forgive her, because Christ had already done that for me. But I wonder what might have happened had I not been praying constantly. See what can happen as you ask for the guidance of the Holy Spirit as you talk to an individual?

One Friday I prepared to leave my office for a weekend speaking date in a nearby Florida city. The heavens opened up and we really had a cloudburst. As a matter of fact, there were tornado warnings for the southern part of the state and I began to doubt the airlines would be flying. This particular weekend I was scheduled on a small independent airline. Many times they have the odd-hour flights that are necessary for me. But the more I listened to the thunder and watched the lightning flash through my office window, the more I wondered if the Lord wanted me up there in one of those little planes.

So I prayed and said, "Praise the Lord, give thanks for all things, because all things work together for good for those that love the Lord. But, Lord, are you sure you want me in one of those little planes? If you do, that's all right with me, because I trust you to get me there safely and I know you want me in Bradenton this weekend."

It continued to pour down and we heard that the highway to the airport was under eight to twelve inches of water. I called the airline to discover that I had been bumped off the small plane for some reason or other and there was no other way to get where I was going except to catch an earlier flight on Eastern. I said, "Praise the Lord, give thanks for all things, because *'all* things work together for good to them that love God.' " I really believe this scripture.

Glancing at the clock, I asked my son, Tom, to drive me to the airport. It was raining so hard I knew I'd never be able to make it. I had to run about ten feet from the office door to get into his car and in those few seconds I was soaked to the skin. Since I was trying to catch an earlier flight than I had anticipated, I knew I wouldn't have time to change my clothes. My son drove to my home a few blocks away where I jumped out to pick up my suit case. Between the first soaking and the few feet of downpour I endured to get into my house, I was completely drenched. My hair, which had just been fixed for the trip, was hanging down in a gummy mess. My suit was completely soaked—did you ever have on a boucle suit when you were really soaked to the skin? (What a mess!) And did you ever start out on a speaking engagement with ink on your hands (if you're in the printing business as I am) because you hadn't had time to wash them since you discovered the only way you could make a speaking engagement was to catch an earlier plane than you had planned to take? Did you ever go sailing off on a speaking tour with runners in your stockings and your work shoes on because you didn't have time to change? Well, I did, and I kept saying, "Thank you, Lord. I don't understand all this, but I know that all things work together for good for those that love the Lord and who are called according to your purpose."

We were so slowed down because of the rain, in spite of my son's driving, I realized we were never going to make the early plane. I just simply prayed, "Lord, you *know* there is no other way for me to get to Bradenton. Please hold that plane on the ground until we get to the airport. And you know it's such bad driving because of the weather we can't possibly make it on time."

Well, I'm firmly convinced that God controls the airlines, too, because when we finally got to the Miami International Airport eleven minutes after takeoff time, you'd never guess what! Or would you? The plane was still on the ground, and the takeoff time had been moved to 4:30! I raced to the counter and was told there were no available seats, only standby. And I was the forty-first standby.

I said, "Thank you, Lord. *All* things work together for good for those who love the Lord." Then I continued, "But you know the only way I can get to Bradenton now is to take this plane to a nearby airport, so you'd better figure out a way to get me around all these standbys."

Soggy mess that I was, I stood there believing that God wanted me to get to a speaking engagement for a church that had called me. I just *knew*—having prayed in faith believing, and constantly rejoicing and giving thanks for all things—that they were going to call me as one of the fortunate standbys. Now don't ask me why, because I don't really understand how God works, I just *believe* that he does. I was the first standby called. There were only a few of us called, and I was the first of those called.

This really excited me, and I got on the plane in great anticipation, because I just *knew* that God wanted me on this plane for a very good reason. Surely, I thought, there must be someone on this particular plane God has prepared just for me to talk to. I sat down and couldn't wait to start the conversation. I happened to have the seat in between two men and I wondered which one it was. I said, "Lord, which one is it whose heart you've prepared?"

Although I didn't get an answer, I tried to start a

conversation with a man on my right. Talk about a brick wall! I really ran into one (and for those who think I never do, believe me when I tell you that I do.) Well, after a few minutes, I knew it wasn't that one, so I decided to attack for the army of Jesus Christ on the left side of me. If I had run into a brick wall on the right side of me, the left side was a solid stone wall. I said, "Well, Lord, now what?"

I was really a wrinkled mess with gummy hair by the time I got to my destination, so I called the pastor of the church where I was to speak. He told me I was over an hour and a half away by limousine. He told me to take one as quickly as possible. I ran outside and was told the limousine had just left. I said, "Praise the Lord," and discovered I'd have to wait thirty minutes for the next limousine to leave.

Then I decided I'd better call the pastor in Bradenton to tell him not to worry because I was really on my way. So I got out of the limousine, made the call and returned to find three young men in the limousine. We left for Bradenton and before we had driven five blocks I knew *why* all the things had happened to me that afternoon to keep me from being on my scheduled trip. And it was not the heart of anyone on the plane that God had prepared, but he had put three young men from three different walks of life together in a limousine with a real Christian fanatic!

The very first sentence spoken gave me an opportunity to share my faith with a young Jewish lawyer, a soldier just returning from Viet Nam, and a student at a Christian school who was really "turned off" on Christ. I began praying as I talked because I knew that God had done a marvelous job before I arrived on the scene, and all he wanted was an available mouth he could use.

I shared what Christ had done in my life, and it was almost eerie how the spirit of God so enveloped that limousine. I was praying and sharing, and sharing and praying, because I could see here were three young men who really needed the Lord. They asked question after question and the Lord provided the necessary answers.

Suddenly the driver of the limousine said, "Mrs. Gardner, you've got five minutes before the first passenger gets out!"

I said, "Thank you, my *brother*," because I knew that God had sent me a brother in Christ to back me up as a prayer warrior for these souls, and now he was telling me if I was going to ask them to pray and ask Christ into their lives, I only had five minutes to wrap it up. I really redoubled my hot line to heaven, and asked them all to bow their heads because I was going to pray a very simple, sinner's prayer, asking God to forgive their sins and asking Christ to come into their hearts and to live his life through each one of them. I said if this was the desire of their heart, to pray the prayer silently after me as I prayed. The atmosphere in that limousine was so God-filled, none of us could deny his presence.

Then as we finished praying, from the lips of the driver came the entire third chapter of John in the most beautiful and Christlike manner I've ever heard. The Holy Spirit of God so filled everyone there that no one made a sound until the driver finished. Then he said, "I'm a retired minister. I was in the ministry for forty-seven years, and I never heard anyone get in a limousine and start talking about Christ the very first sentence and never stop!" I almost cracked up because here was an ordained minister of God, but you know what? God had sent him to back up the job He had assigned to me.

And would you believe that one of the young men had been bumped off the same airline I had. He said now he understood why. The young soldier just returning from Viet Nam said he realized now why God had spared him in combat. The Jewish lawyer did not pray to receive Christ, but the Holy Spirit was really dealing with him because the tears were streaming down his cheeks.

Need I tell you what happened in the church where I was scheduled to speak? In spite of all my messy clothes, my gummy hair, my hands full of ink, my everything that wasn't the way it should have been, I prayed "Lord, don't let them see *me*. Let them see only Christ living his life through me so they won't notice any of these little details."

God answered that prayer, too. The excitement of what had happened to me because I had trusted God and believed his word rubbed off all over that congregation! Read that verse in I Thessalonians again and see if it doesn't take on a different meaning. "Rejoice *always*, pray *constantly, give thanks in all circumstances;* for this is the will of God in Christ Jesus for you."

See what happens when you do!

CHAPTER 7

## PRAY FOR EVERYTHING

*Again I say to you, if two of you agree on earth about anything they ask, it will be done for them by my Father in heaven.*
—Matthew 18:19-20

PROBABLY one of the most exciting proofs of this verse took place on a tour I made to California. This entire trip was the result of prayer, and God guided every step of the way. God is so completely interested in every area of our lives, I often wonder why we don't invite him to give us the correct answers to *every* problem we have. As I told you previously, I used to think we had to reserve God for the BIG things. And then I discovered that because God is interested in our complete life, we can ask him for help with the smallest details.

I didn't know why I felt called to California, but I never question why either. I just knew that God called me to go to California, so I made plans to go. First, I must explain something. I go at a tremendous pace all the time. Between speaking engagements, running a printing company, trying to manage a home, plus having an active part in my own church, I really am on the GO! I serve a King, and I believe, as an ambassador to a King, I should look as much like a queen as possible.

In the back of my mind I had hidden the thought that I would get some new clothes before I went west. I never seem to have enough time to go clothes shopping. Not only that, I really despise shopping because it seems such a waste of time to me. To further complicate matters, at this writing I happen to be a size eighteen and it's not the easiest thing in the world to get sharp looking clothes for anyone who wears that big a size. I really think most clothes manufacturers hate the big woman. They either make us look dowdy or so matronly it's awful.

Well, about a week before I was to leave for California I still didn't have any new clothes. Did I panic? No, I did not. I just prayed. And would you honestly like to know how I prayed? I said, "Lord, you don't want me to go to California looking like a slob, do you? As your personal representative do you want me to wear my worn out clothes? And you know I just don't have time to go shopping before I go. So, Lord, would you please solve this problem and see that I get some new clothes?"

Would *you* honestly pray for new clothes? Would

you honestly believe that God would answer a request of this kind? I hope you will look back at the paragraph above and see my reason for asking for the new clothes. I'm sure if I had said, "Lord, you know how much I love clothes and how much they mean to me," the Lord would have ignored my request. But my only desire was to look like an ambassador to a King. And safe and secure in the knowledge that he would answer my request, I tore back through the mountain of work on my desk, knowing that I had nothing to worry about. The next morning I got a call from a friend who said, "Frances, do you have your new clothes for your trip to California?"

I silently said, "Thank you, Lord," because I knew here was the answer. To her I said, "No, I haven't had time to get them yet."

And she said, "Well, I just started to work at a new dress shop and they had a fashion show last Saturday (what good does a size 5 or 7 do me? I wondered) and the models were size eighteen. The dresses used in the fashion show are marked down 50 per cent because they were worn." I tore out of the office, got into my car, and while saying "Thank you, Lord, for working out even the smallest of details," I drove over to the store. Within an hour and a half I had selected not just one outfit, but ten stunning outfits—enough for an entire speaking year—and most of them half price, too! You might think it extravagant to buy ten outfits at one time, but I have learned first hand that traveling and speaking are about the hardest things I know of on clothes. It's thrilling to me to know God cares what I look like!

I had a speaking engagement the night I left for California, so my son went with me and drove me directly to the airport afterward. I then started one of the most exciting, prayerful trips of my life. The actual plane trip to California was uneventful. The only passengers on the plane were three other men, so we all slept on the flight. When we landed in California, it was at an unearthly hour—around 3 A.M.—so I went to a motel for the balance of the night (or morning). I was due at noon that day in Fullerton, California.

I had never been to the Los Angeles Airport, so had no idea how big and how confusing it was to a real stranger. I had lived briefly in California during the war years (my children say it was the Civil War, but it was really World War II), but things change a lot in twenty-five years, so I was really a stranger.

I was to be the guest of Helen Kooiman, author of *Cameos, Women Fashioned by God,* that first day at the Fullerton Christian Woman's Club. Not knowing anything about the commuter plane service in Los Angeles I decided to go to the airport, find out what time the plane was leaving, and then call Helen and tell her when and where she could meet me. After getting lost in the huge airport because the cab driver let me off at the wrong commuter airline, I boarded a little jitney bus with five suitcases, etc. and after arriving at the correct airline asked what time the next plane left for Fullerton. The answer: "In three minutes. If you'll run, we'll hold the plane for you."

A porter grabbed my luggage, and we started running as fast as I could (and that's not very fast). I said, "Lord, please don't let me have a heart attack before I get to share what Christ has done in my life." I promptly slowed down and made it safely to the little commuter plane.

I had arrived in California during what I'm sure was the monsoon season, because I never saw so much rain in my entire life. The commuter planes are quite small and when we got up in the air, I realized how hard it was raining and how little the plane was. Then I peeked out the window and saw the Pacific Ocean below me (and not very far below me at that) and the lightning and the rain. I said, "Lord, if you want me splaaaat all over the place, that's all right with me, but if it's all the same to you, would you please get this little plane safely to Fullerton?"

And then I relaxed, knowing that God was in control of the situation. It takes about twenty minutes to fly from Los Angeles to Fullerton. And about half way through the trip, I realized that in my haste I had not called Helen. I also knew if she didn't meet me I'd have no way of getting to the Christian Woman's Club on time. Again I called on the power of God, and I prayed: "Lord, Helen's *got to know* that I have arrived in California, and that I am on this plane. In the way that only you can do, will you please let my sister in Christ know that I am on *this* plane."

Now go with me to Helen's house. She had been taking care of last minute details, knowing I would be in sometime that day. Then she sat down to eat her breakfast. Being a great prayer warrior, she asked God to give me a safe trip to California. But before she could begin to eat her breakfast, God's Holy Spirit communicated with her. She pushed back her grapefruit, saying she was compelled to go to the telephone and call Catalina Airlines to find out when their next plane was due in. They said "in exactly ten minutes."

Helen said, "Thank you, Lord, for letting me know Frances is on that plane." She slipped on a raincoat, took an umbrella, ran to her car, and drove to the airport where we greeted each other as if we both had known exactly all the details.

After we loaded the car and were driving to her home, she said, "Did you pray about ten minutes before the plane landed that I would meet you?" Goosepimples covered me as I realized that God's Holy Spirit had rendezvoused as our spirits had witnessed with each other. Could this be mere coincidence? I hope you believe God answered prayer!

And while God was busy answering prayers up and down the coast of California, he was also taking care of my personal affairs in Florida. For many years I had lived in a big home: eight rooms, three baths, swimming pool; and for my first three Christian years, the Lord had used my home as a halfway house. I was privileged to have many young people share the hospitality and Christian love in my home. There were times when we had four or five extra people living with us, but now it seemed the Lord was indicating the time for the big house was past.

I was spending more and more of my time on speaking trips, and my real family at home consisted of one teenage daughter who goes with me whenever possible, so I guess the Lord decided we didn't need the expense or worry of a big house, so he laid on my heart the desire to sell it. If anyone had ever told me I would ever sell this house, I would have said, "Never!" This was the home where my daughter was brought from the hospital; the house where the orchids from my wedding bouquet are embedded in concrete under the window; the home where I lived when Christ became a reality in my life; the home where hundreds had been introduced to Christ; where new Christians had learned to pray; where lives had been transformed because of the way the Lord was using me. But I guess as we grow in Christ he advances us or says "Now you're ready for this," or, "I want to use you in this area." I never question what God has for me. I only know that he's much smarter than I, and anything he has planned for me is far better than anything I can concoct.

Just as I left for California, I listed the house with a real estate broker, and prayed, "Lord, if you want me to sell this house, sell it while I'm in California so I won't be hurt if someone says 'I don't like this. I don't like that!' "

The second day I was in California I received a call

with an offer on the house. Two days later I had two bonafide offers for the house, both of which were for the price I had asked. I believe that God is also in the real estate business! How could I doubt it?

I signed the papers out in California, and returned home at the end of three weeks to discover I had exactly sixteen days in which to relocate. Do you realize how much you can accumulate after living in the same house for sixteen years? And to be told you have sixteen days to get out, knowing how much you have to do, would panic even the most self-sufficient person. But I'm so glad I'm *not* self-sufficient. When I heard this exciting news, I said, "Lord, you know the housing situation in Miami—there just aren't enough apartments to rent—and yet I know this is what you wanted. So now, Lord, I'll have to lay all my needs before you."

My needs were several: I had to consider being near the high school my daughter attends. I have, as a working mother, always felt my home had to be within walking distance of my office, so that my children could get to me any time they needed me. Along with these considerations, I had enlarged my office and was in the process of moving an established business, so the new home had to be close to my new office location.

I hope you don't think I pushed the panic button, because I didn't. When I put that request to God, I turned my hand over with the palm down, and dropped my arm to my side. I went out and got in the car and said, "Lord, you know I'm swamped with responsibilities and serving you, so please direct my car to where you want us to live." With complete confidence that the fabulous God I serve had the situation completely under control, I started out.

Again you may say it's coincidence, but the Lord directed my car to a street where they were building some new duplexes. I had not felt led to buy another home, but felt the temporary answer was an apartment.

I got out of the car and asked if there were any available and what the price was. The rent was exactly what I had figured I could afford, but the duplexes were all rented; however, there was *one* about completed and which was not rented yet. And do you know the completion date? The completion date on the new apartment was the day I had to vacate my house. God is even in the apartment rental business!

Well, back to California now, to share some more prayer experiences out there! It had rained every day I was in California—and I mean it really poured! Beautiful homes were caught in mud slides and went into the canyons, disaster was rampant. I couldn't help but feel the raindrops were God's tears spilling because of the spiritual state of his people. Nevertheless God was granting harvest after harvest as I shared his exciting word.

I had been scheduled to go to San Diego but, because of the flood waters, all the freeways except one were closed. Travel on that one wasn't advisable because it was covered in places with water. But my publisher's salesman, his wife, and I prayed, asking God to see that the road was safe for us to travel to San Diego. As we drove along the freeway, we sang "Heavenly Sunshine, *flooding* my soul with glory divine." And then we really cracked up, because as we sang "*flooding,*" all we could see was water, with just a ribbon of highway down the middle.

Many people had asked me if I had prayed that the rains would stop, but, strangely, I couldn't pray this request. It just wasn't a burden on my heart, so I had truthfully answered each time "No!"

We got to San Diego in midafternoon and after speaking that night, I retired sensing a great burden to pray that the rain would stop. It had rained some sixty days in a row, but I felt *now* was the time to pray for the sun, and so I asked God for just a little of nature's sunshine since he had been so bountiful with his heavenly sunshine. And I went to bed—eager to face the sunrise.

I was scheduled to be on a telecast the next morning, so I got up early and went over to the TV station. I talked for a few minutes to the performers on the program. Before leaving the hotel room I had asked God to make me a blessing to someone that day and to really prepare a heart he wanted me to talk to. The exciting thing is I never know whose heart it's going to be! And I certainly wasn't prepared for what the Lord did that day with my prayer request. I talked to the star of the show, to the weather girl, and to the newscaster.

One thing I've learned is that a Christian rarely fares well on a secular program, especially a "silly old Christian lady." Christians usually come on when the peacock is preening so you can get your color set tuned in correctly. And by the time the host asks, "What is your name?" and "What in the world are you doing here?" the Christian is off the program, and that's the end.

But this particular morning as I talked to the star I could sense God at work, because the man turned and said to the production manager, "Put her on last!" Last spot is the star spot, I thought. And I prayed, "Lord, you really take care of things in a great way, don't you?"

Interestingly enough, as I talked to the host of the show, I became aware that in his life there was a God-shaped vacuum that had not yet been filled by a personal relationship with Jesus Christ. He had asked me about the weather, and with complete faith, I replied, "I don't think it's going to rain today, because for the first time since I've been in California I felt led to pray that the rain would stop."

Now notice what happened! The show started, and the weather girl said the weather man predicted rain. Then the M.C. said a most surprising thing. He said, "We have this morning a guest who wrote a book called *God Is Fabulous*. She has just told me she asked God to let us have a little sunshine. What do you think about that?"

The weather girl said, "Mr. Weatherman says 'rain' today and he's *never* wrong."

The M.C. asked the newscaster what he thought about my prayer, and he said, "I'll reserve my opinion." I thought, God is using people today to bring home a point.

The entire show was exciting, and I watched and enjoyed all the guests on the program, all the while mentally visualizing how I was really going to ham it up. I could just see all the producers in Hollywood running after me to film the story of my life—but God had other plans.

When it came my turn to be on the show, I looked at the M.C. and all I could see was a gaping hole in his life that needed to be filled. From that moment I could not have cared less what anyone on television thought about me. I only knew a soul needed spiritual help. It was probably the most peculiar interview ever on television: a searching heart God had prepared talking to the one sent to be the harvester.

As I talked I was also earnestly praying, and just before the program was over, the star said to me, "What do I have to do to get what you've got?" Again spiritual goosepimples crawled up and down my back, and my heart leaped. Time was up, so I just blurted out, "Pray and ask Christ to come into your heart and ask God to forgive your sins!" The weather girl came back on for the final weather report, and I noticed she had changed the forecast "rain" to "fair." She commented she had looked out the window and it looked clear.

I was scheduled to speak at the Christian Business Men's Club at lunch that day, so as soon as the TV program was over, I said "I want you at the CBM luncheon today."

The M.C. replied, "Can't make it, sorry!"

I said, "Oh, yes you can!" (All the while I was silently praying.) And then I had to leave because I was scheduled to be on a radio program. It just so happened this was a Christian Broadcasting Station and, after an exciting hour-long program, I told the young man who interviewed me about the TV program. I said, "Pray that he'll make it to the luncheon."

Roger said, "Let's pray right now." There were three of us there: the radio station manager, a Christian bookstore owner, and I.

We formed a prayer circle and first the radio station manager prayed: "Lord, see that Bob gets to that luncheon today. Make whatever changes are necessary in his schedule to see that he makes it to that luncheon. We thank you *right* now for answered prayer and we just can't wait to see him there."

Then it was my turn. And since the Bible says, "If two of you agree on earth about anything they ask, it will be done for them by my Father in heaven," and since God knew I was agreeing with my prayer partner, I didn't have to repeat the request. So I prayed like this: "Lord, thank you for sending Bob to the luncheon, and this day we claim his soul for the kingdom of God. Send your Holy Spirit to convict him so that he can join the royal family of God. And Lord, how we thank you because of what you promise."

We almost ran to the luncheon after that. And can you guess who was the second one there? You're right, Bob was. So I prayed, "Thank you, Lord, for sending Bob to the luncheon." I don't believe I ever ate or talked so fast as I did that day. At the end I gave everyone there an opportunity to pray and receive Christ. As I finished, I walked over to Bob and said,

"Did you pray to receive Christ when I said the prayer at the end?"

He said, "I *think* I did when you prayed on TV this morning."

"Not good enough," I said, "You've got to *know* that you asked Christ into your life." Then I said, "Where is Christ right now?"

He replied, "I *think* he's in my heart!"

I said, "Not good enough. You've got to *know* he's in your heart!" Seeing my prayer partner, Roger, from the radio station, I said, "Let's pray that God will give Bob the assurance he needs."

We prayed, and after I had prayed, I heard Bob's voice say one of the simplest prayers I've ever heard, but never have I heard one with so much feeling. He very simply said in tones that tore my heart into pieces, "O Christ, *I want you in my life.*" Tears welled up and rolled down his cheeks and splattered on the floor as God's Holy Spirit melted him and took him into his royal family.

Three of us prayed *specifically* in faith believing, and see what happened? Try it!

# CHAPTER 8

# PRAY "RIGHT NOW"

*And it shall come to pass, that before they call, I will answer; and while they are yet speaking, I will hear.*

—Isaiah 65:24

Do YOU have an urgency for praying? One of the greatest mistakes in anyone's prayer life is to not pray when the need, desire, urge, or whatever-you-want-to-call-it is there. When someone asks you to pray for him, do you slough him off with "I'll pray for you"? This is grossly unfair to the person, who apparently has a great need or he wouldn't ask you to pray. And, really, it isn't fair to God, who hears while you are yet speaking. His Word says so.

Right now I'm thinking of many times when I've been asked to pray for various individuals. If God's Holy Spirit says "Pray right now," I stop whatever I'm doing, wherever I am, and say, "Let's pray right now!" I believe when a person is desperate enough to ask someone else to pray for him, it's an urgent need and I'm reminded that God wants to answer before we finish speaking. But how can he answer when we fail to even get started because we aren't willing to pray right now?

I was weekending in a church in northern Ohio where one of the great burdens of the church was for a young man who for years had come close to God, then backed off. He attended a men's breakfast the church gave, and then at lunch I met his fiance. She shared with me the great concern for his soul and I could feel the earnestness and sincerity of her desire as she asked me to pray that God's Holy Spirit would speak to him at the Sunday service. So I said, "Let's pray *right now!*" We were at a buffet luncheon, so we both put our trays down *right there,* clasped hands, were joined by a third woman who had overheard her request, and the three of us stood right there and fervently prayed that God would redeem her fiance in the Sunday morning service. Spiritual goosepimples flew up and down the spines of all of us because of the extreme fervency of the moment.

I could hardly wait for the Sunday morning service. When the invitation was given, this woman's fiance was the first one to come forward to give his heart to the Lord. I have often wondered what would have happened if we had not stopped right at the moment of request to pray as we did.

Would I have remembered to pray that night when I went to bed? Or might I have forgotten? Would the fervency of the prayer have been as great had I prayed alone hours later as it was when we prayed "right now"? Would I have prayed as sincerely as I did at the moment when I felt the great urgency? Might I have not forgotten all about the request and not even given God an opportunity to answer that prayer? I believe so. And do you have any idea what happened to the prayer of the women who attended that luncheon and who overheard the prayers we made? Imagine what happened to them as they saw proof positive that God answers prayers!

I visited for a weekend in another church, where attendance had been extremely poor. The few who attended were not very exciting Christians and were *posi-*

*tive* they couldn't get anyone to come to church with them. One woman said "I'm lucky I get myself here, let alone someone else!"

The pastor and I felt the situation required some real fast praying, so we prayed, and asked God to lead us to homes where the people would be receptive to our visit and would come to church as a result of the visit. After praying right on the spot, we took off on an unscheduled tour of homes, stopping briefly to share a little of God's love, and then on to the next house. In the last home where we stopped there was an alcoholic mother. The daughter called me into her bedroom to look at something. When I went in, she became almost hysterical and said, "Please pray that my mother will get to church so that she can be saved!" We prayed right on the spot . . . only a very short, but very earnest and fervent, prayer because we knew we couldn't be gone too long. Shortly after that, the pastor and I left.

When it was time for the church service to start, the pastor and I looked into the sanctuary and this particular family was not there. We had prayed at the dinner table and asked God to be sure they were there, but since they weren't, we withdrew into a side room and prayed specifically for this family. When we went out the door, we saw them being seated in the sanctuary.

Well, I know what you're going to say: How could God have answered that prayer when they must have already been on the church parking lot? You know how? God knew we were going to pray fervently and specifically for them and so he said, "before they call, I will answer." His Holy Spirit had moved on this family even before we had called out, therefore he answered our prayer.

Over and over I have prayed with people moments after they have asked me to pray for something, little realizing I would say, "Let's pray *right now!*" I have had the thrill of seeing God answer these prayers in a matter of hours. *We have not, because we ask not.* And one of the reasons we ask not is because most of us are procrastinators. We keep putting things off. As a result of this, many prayers never get answered because they never get prayed. We get too busy and too involved in other things and just don't take time out to pray.

On a trip to California I was privileged to be the guest of Mary Ann Mooney, a great Christian leader. She gave a coffee for me while I was there. We had prayed fervently for the results of this coffee, asking that God would bring many who needed Christ. The morning of the coffee we began to hear of great numbers of persons who were coming. At first we were fearful of having too many for the size of the house, but then we yielded our fears and Mary Ann and I went into the closet (literally) and prayed that God would send so many there would be standing room only! God heard, and answered, "while they are yet speaking, I will hear."

Recently at a weekend visit to a midwestern church I was asked to talk to a real drunkard, husband of one of the members. I knew nothing about the situation except that everyone had been praying for this man. As we parked the car, I asked the minister to pray with me. In just two or three short sentences we claimed the man's soul for the kingdom of God. When we had finished, I sent up my own special prayer and said, "Lord, I can't do it, and you know it, so just prepare his heart right now. Then give me the words you'd have me to say."

Since people seem to think an author or speaker has a magic wand or something to wave, this very fact, perhaps more than anything else, has caused me to pray most fervently, asking the Lord's help because of the responsibility placed on me. A verse which comes to me over and over tells the whole story. "Not by might, nor by power, but by my *Spirit,* saith the Lord."

# CHAPTER 9

# PRAY AT THE BEGINNING OF THE ROPE

*The eyes of the Lord are toward the righteous, and his ears toward their cry. The face of the Lord is against evildoers, to cut off the remembrance of them from the earth. When the righteous cry for help, the Lord hears, and delivers them out of all their troubles.* —Psalm 34:15-17

SOME OF the most rewarding, thrilling verses in the Bible are found in the psalms. They are also most soothing—the kind you need to read when you've had a bad day and things just aren't going right. There's something about the beauty of the psalms that comfort like nothing else does.

I often think of Psalm 34:17, which reads, "When the righteous cry for help, the Lord hears, and delivers them out of all their troubles." It is wonderful to know that to those who love the Lord he is faithful to deliver from all troubles. But this verse also brings to my mind a question: Why do we always wait until we get to the "end of our rope"? I was listening to a testimony service one night in a church I visited. Almost everyone who testified told of a great prayer answer, but almost every testimony contained the same words. "When I got to the end of my rope, I said, 'Lord, I can't do it. Help me! Help me!' and the Lord delivered me."

God wants us to know that we are totally dependent upon him. "Trust in the Lord with all thine heart; and lean not unto thine own understanding" (Proverbs 3:5). He wants us to love him and trust him so much we rely upon him for every need of life. I often wonder why ego or self always tries to do it first without God. Then when we get to the end of the rope we scream and cry out for God to deliver us. Just think of the fact that all the time we are struggling to do it ourselves, God patiently waits to hear us cry out to him to help us. I wonder how often he must be saddened when he sees us making such a mess of our lives, refusing to call upon him, when he wants to do so much for us.

My daughter went on a vacation where she found she was completely without Christian fellowship. She immediately turned to her Bible and began reading and studying more than she ever had before. And she began to pray more than she ever had before.

Being lonesome, she called me long distance and said, "Mother, I can't stand it without Christian fellowship, so would you please just have a prayer time with me over the telephone." We prayed for about twenty minutes over long distance telephone. Do you think I complained about the cost of that prayer? I *did not,* because she was smart enough to want to do something at the beginning of the rope instead of waiting until she was desperate and at the end of the rope.

One of the greatest ways to improve your prayer life is to be the "beginning of the rope" for others. Do you ever take on the prayer burdens of other people? You'd be surprised to discover how this will turn your thoughts away from yourself, and how much stronger your prayer life will be because you are picking up that rope for others.

While we're thinking about picking up the rope for

others, I'd like to make a suggestion you may want to try. I remember how when I first became a Christian, my pastor suggested I make out a prayer list. I thought he was insane because to read the prayer list I knew I'd have to peek. Of course, I didn't think it was fair if you opened your eyes while praying. And anyway, I couldn't imagine anyone having so many things to pray about they had to be written down in a book, but finally I learned. And if you really want to discover the power of prayer, and discover how God really answers prayer, I'd like to suggest that you develop a prayer group. Since a group is any number more than two, you can regulate the size of your group by yourself. I think five or six are enough persons to have in a prayer cell.

If you're a new Christian, or you're not too strong in your faith, I'd suggest you get a couple of good prayer warriors in the group with you. How often you meet depends upon your needs and your personalities. Some people like to go to a prayer warrior meeting every Thursday morning at 10 A.M. I like to have a prayer meeting whenever there is a need. But in the beginning it might be worthwhile to have a certain designated time to meet each week. The only problem I find with this is either the devil comes in and tries to give everybody umpteen reasons for not attending, or people get frustrated by being tied down every week at the same time for the same purpose.

Because there is a need to start somewhere, suppose you have a prayer meeting every Thursday morning. If you have access to inexpensive printing, you might have some prayer request books made up. If not, just buy some regular 8½x11 inch paper and have everyone make his own prayer book. Have the paper cut lengthwise down the middle to make 4¼x11 inch strips. Take perhaps ten of these pieces, fold them in half to make them 4¼ x 5½ inches and then staple in the middle. You might want to put a little heavier paper on the outside to strengthen the book. Then across each page make these headings:

*Date*          *Prayer Request*          *Date Answered*

(Note: Do not write the entire request down, but just enough so that you remember what to pray for.) Your requests might be something like this:

5/22   Patience for Mary in dealing with her children.
       Prepare heart of Sue's husband.
       Joe not walking close to God.
       Healing touch for Aunt Rose.
       Give more love to Ann in dealing with people.
       Curb the critical spirit in Jane.
       Gene's son is on dope.
       Soul of Bob.
       Need fourteen more workers for Vacation Bible
          School.
       Need new organist for church since ours is being
          transferred.

5/29   Pray for transportation for Howard to school.
       Desperate. Urgent.
       Urgently need more people for visitation pro-
          gram.
       Enthusiastic youth leaders (preferably a cou-
          ple).
       Pastor.

Now the fun and excitement really begin. After you ask around the circle what the prayer requests are, then ask each person in the circle to pray for each request. You will notice that each of the requests I have listed tells only a small portion of the story. You have no idea what this will do to people in opening up avenues of prayer, because each will see a different need and a different way to pray for each of these different subjects. Each of the different prayers will be of help to the individual being prayed for, and will certainly be enrichment to all who are sitting there in accord with the one who is praying.

Next week, as soon as your group meets, get out your prayer request-and-answer books and ask who had a prayer answered. Let me assure you they won't all be answered in one week, but you might find under the "Date Answered" column this notation the first week: Sue's husband accepted Christ 6/6. Or: 6/9—Last of the fourteen volunteers for Vacation Bible School came forth.

After this, if no more prayers were answered this week, ask for new requests for the next week. As you add them to the list, express gratitude and praise to God for the two definite prayer answers this week. Next week you might find that Gene's son has been miraculously delivered from the dope habit, a new organist came to church and asked if he could be of service, or Joe really took stock of himself and is back in close fellowship with God again.

At the end of three months, review your prayer book. You will be absolutely amazed at the number of definite and positive answers to prayer that you have received.

Don't ever throw out an old prayer book, though, because three years from the time you put a prayer request in your book, you might discover that God answered your prayer. The reason I say this is because more than three years ago I wrote in the prayer book of a Gideon a request concerning the soul of a loved one. Three years later I had the fun of dropping him a note and telling him the date that request had been answered. You can imagine what that did for him to know that God had answered a prayer request even if it was three years old!

You might even become a "request collector." There

are many people who have great burdens and would love to have someone earnestly pray for them. Keep your prayer book handy in your automobile, purse (if you're a woman) or suit pocket (if you're a man). Anytime you see someone who might begin casually discussing a problem with you, ask if you can pray for him. You don't know what it will do for that person to know that you are interested. And you don't know what it will do for your prayer life either. Did you ever realize that God is just waiting with his arms outstretched and hands filled with prayer answers for you? He says, "Call unto me, and I will answer thee, and show thee great and mighty things, which thou knowest not" (Jer. 34:3). Call to him, right now!

Another advantage of this type of prayer, as opposed to praying alone all the time, is that it gives you love and concern for those who are praying with you. This will really enrich your life. There springs up between people who pray together a bond Christian love unequaled by anything I know. There is genuine closeness between people who pray together, and if, for some reason, you have a rather "blah" feeling toward prayer some morning, you will be caught up in the fervency of someone else's prayers.

I recall several women in my church who have been in the same prayer circle with me and who have prayer books with the same requests as mine. I have for each one of them a special feeling which I know is the result of our praying and rejoicing together as we have seen the hot line to heaven really work!

# CHAPTER 10

# LEARN TO ABIDE

*But if you live your life in me, and my
words live in your hearts, you can ask for
whatever you like and it will come true
for you.* —John 15:7, Phillips

*If you abide in me, and my words abide
in you, ask whatever you will, and it shall
be done for you.* —John 15:7

IF THERE is a secret to "successful" prayer, it is found in
John 15:7. As I have studied various scriptures concerning prayer I have become aware of one outstanding
fact. Almost all of them have a requirement! "If you
have faith as a grain of mustard seed," "Whatever you
ask in prayer . . . if you have faith." "But let him ask in
faith, with no doubting." "If two of you agree on earth
about anything. . . ." "Take delight in the Lord." Look
at each one of these verses and think of the requirement
imposed upon you.

I especially like "Take delight in the Lord, and he
will give you the desires of your heart." What a marvelous thought, but the condition or requirement is a steep
one because it says we must first meet his requirement
of taking delight in the Lord. Taking delight in the
Lord, to me, is to share him with everyone I meet, saying "Praise the Lord," basking in his great and mighty

love, and letting people know I'm loving every minute of it. That's "taking delight" in the Lord!

Now here's the true test. If your prayer life has been unsatisfactory and you feel God doesn't really answer your prayers, think honestly about John 15:7. Does "if you *abide* in me, and my words abide in you," apply to you? Do you really abide in the Lord? Do his words really *abide* in you? Webster says abide means "to rest, to dwell, to continue permanently, or in the same state; *to be firm and immovable."* And then going on to the word *abiding,* there are many interesting synonyms such as "continuing, lasting, enduring, durable, steadfast, changeless, remaining, awaiting."

Think of God's "abiding" love. Let's substitute each of the above adjectives. God's "continuing" love; God's "lasting" love; God's "enduring" love; God's "durable" love; God's "steadfast" love; God's "changeless" love; God's "remaining" love; God's "awaiting" love. Every one of these words in conjunction with God's love causes chills to run up and down my spine.

If you want to use the same words in a little different order, try them this way: Are you "continuing" in God; are you "steadfast" in God's love; are you "changeless" in God's love; are you "remaining" in God's love, are you "awaiting" God's love? Sitting right where you are, just imagine that you are "awaiting" God's love. What a tremendous thought. Just think about the possibilities behind that little statement.

And so to me it seems the door to God's prayer answers hinges on our "abiding" in Christ. It really seems so simple, because Christ doesn't really leave much to imagination. He specifically says "if you abide in me, and my words abide in you, *ask whatever you will,* and it shall be done for you." What in the world is the matter with the Christian world today? Do we really believe what God says? If we really believe what God says in his word, then why don't we claim his promises to us?

Why don't we take advantage of the fact that he says, "*Ask whatever you will*, and it shall be done for you"? Many people are really afraid to step out in faith and claim this promise. It's so exciting to me to realize that God is here, right now, just waiting for a prayer request to answer.

The Phillips translation might make it easier to understand. In today's language it says, "But if you *live* your life in me, and my words *live* in your hearts, *you can ask for whatever you like and it will come true for you.*" All Christ asks is that we *live* our lives in him, and let his words *live* in our hearts, or let his words be *alive* in our hearts. He doesn't say a word about living just a tiny little bit of your life for him, he simply says to live your entire life for him.

Again Webster brings an interesting fact to mind in the definition of the word life—"that property of plants and animals which makes it possible for them to take in food, get energy from it, grow, adapt themselves to their surroundings, and reproduce their kind: *it is the quality that distinguishes a living animal or plant from inorganic matter or a dead organism.*"

Probably the biggest secret anyone could share on prayer is just learn to "abide" in Christ and then see what happens to your prayer life.

Look at 1 John 3:22. "And whatsoever we ask, we receive of him, *because we keep his commandments, and do those things that are pleasing in his sight.*"* How can we be pleasing in his sight unless we "abide" in him at all times. I wonder why we work so hard for all the material things that can keep us from doing the things that are pleasing in his sight. This keeps us from claiming his promise that *whatsoever we ask, we* receive of him. Why do we run after money, fame, excitement, thrills, when it would be so much

*Italics are the author's.

simpler to just believe in God, abide in him, and whatsoever we ask, we shall receive. If we all really believed this with all our hearts and souls, we wouldn't have worry and frustrations, because he would grant us whatever we asked.

Of course, this goes back to a previous thought which says if we really allow Christ to live his life *through* us, we will not desire or ask for things other than what he wants us to have. And that's the very best, because God wants only the best for his children. He loves us so much.

Look at your own children—if you're a parent. Aren't we much more likely to give them good gifts if they are obedient to us? Certainly we are. And when son or daughter says, "I love you," what do parents do? It makes us want to give them everything that is *best* for them. This must be the way God feels about us when we lift our voices in prayer, telling him how much we love him. He wants us to have our heart's desires. This leads me to inquire into the meaning of prayer.

What is prayer? If you asked me this question, I might list the following:

Prayer is an admission that we believe there is a God.

Prayer is just talking to God.

Prayer is praising God for what he has done for you.

Prayer is listening to God to find out his will for your life.

Prayer is the way God talks to you.

Prayer is a two-way street between just you and God.

Prayer is a heavenly communication system.

Prayer is that which removes you from the "worldly" world and transports you to a spiritual world.

Prayer is asking God to show you what he wants you to do.

Prayer is how we reach God and how God reaches us.

Prayer is the way we ask for miracles for others.

If we did not believe in the reality of God, would we

pray to just thin air? I don't believe so. Whether you are a Christian or not, when you pray, you are actually admitting that God exists and you believe he exists. Otherwise you would not be taking time out to pray to a non-existent thing or being.

Prayer is a great cleansing compound for our minds. Take time out to pray and see if you have time for evil thoughts when you've been occupied with thoughts of and for and from God. There just isn't any room.

Prayer is a great source of power. Did you ever see an entire church pray fervently in unity for something? You can almost physically feel the power of prayer.

Prayer gives you the ability to stand alone with God. You can be physically alone anywhere in the whole world yet, through prayer, immediately discover that you are no longer alone. God, through his Son, Jesus Christ, is right there with you. Have you ever felt more alone than when you were on an operating table awaiting surgery? And yet, have you ever felt closer to God, as you began to pray in a situation like this?

Prayer is the remover of guilt. Perhaps, before you became a Christian, the problem of guilt was real in your life. In some people the feeling of guilt is greater than in others, but it is present in every life until we ask Christ to cleanse us and forgive our sins. Prayer removes guilt from your life because God's Word says, "He is faithful and just to cleanse us from all unrighteousness."

Prayer is the answer to loneliness. Have you ever been all alone in a strange city, or even in your own home town and be overcome with loneliness? I remember years ago the strangling feeling of loneliness when I was alone. Yet no longer am I alone, because I know through prayer I can always eliminate any feeling of loneliness by inviting Christ to be near me.

I have often been asked if it shows lack of faith to pray over and over for the same request. There have been times in my life (and this is most of the time) when I pray only once for a certain thing, because if I am in tune with God, I just *know* my prayer has been answered. Stand on the promise of "Ask, and ye shall receive." The Bible simply says "Ask, and it shall be given unto you."

On the other hand we must consider the apostle Paul who prayed three times concerning the "thorn in the flesh." No pat answer can be given here. I'm also reminded of Jesus in the Garden of Gethsemane. I'm sure he repeated over and over his prayer requests that night. And in Ephesians 6:18, Paul writes, "Pray at all times in the Spirit, with all prayer and supplication." Other versions say "Pray constantly." The only advice I offer in this situation is: if you feel that once is enough, great. If you feel a need or an urge to pray more than once for the same thing, then just keep on praying until you feel in your heart there is no further need to pray.

CHAPTER 11

## SURRENDER ALL

GOD HAS the most unique way of dealing in situations long before we are aware of his plan. All of this book was completed except the last chapter, and for some bewildering reason I could not pick up God's message for the final chapter. That's because it hadn't yet been written, and I had to be patient, knowing that God would reveal what he wanted me to include in this chapter. I wondered as each chapter unfolded why I had dedicated the book to my son, Tom. Yet I had made little mention of him throughout the book. But now I know why. This final chapter contains more prayer than any other chapter in the book since it concerns my own flesh and blood.

Maybe I had better tell you a little about me before I became a Christian to help you better understand the nature of the prayers which make this chapter possible. Thirteen years ago I was left with two children to support. At that time the doctors had pronounced a death sentence upon me, saying I couldn't live over two months. Even though I wasn't a Christian, I knew God answered prayer, so I prayed and asked God to let me live long enough to raise my two children.

Forced by the necessity of providing a living for myself and my two children, I started a secretarial service with fifteen dollars. I made arrangements with the owner of a shopping center to accept office rent in the form of secretarial service from me. Thus started another undercapitalized, "overage" owner business. Everything in the books said I was destined to fail: I had very poor health, I was over forty, I had small children with no one to care for them. There wasn't a reason in the world why I should have succeeded—except that God was working in my life. Many people have asked me what I used the $15.00 for. I spent $5.00 for a ream of bond paper, $5.00 for a ream of onionskin, and $4.95 for a box of carbon paper. I borrowed a typewriter and started my business.

Unbelievably, the business prospered in spite of my undercharging. To make up for undercharging, I started working sixteen to eighteen hours daily, sitting at a typewriter. Hauling a typewriter home at night so I could be with my children, I would spend half of the night typing so I could earn a few extra dollars to feed my children, clothe them, and send my little girl to a private school where she could be taken care of during the day.

The business grew and grew, eventually turning into a printing company. When I first became a Christian I always told my pastor that I was so busy I couldn't come to church on Sunday evenings or Wednesday evenings. He said, "Frances, you can do whatever you *want* to do. But the day you learn to put *first* things *first* in your life, you'll be a lot better off."

All I can say is PTL because from that statement, I learned at least partially how to put first things first in my life, and I never again missed a midweek service, or a Sunday night service. But I still had the great problem of working four or five nights a week until 3 or 4 a.m. trying to catch up on business that had to be done. I see now it was because something drove me to want the business to be a big success!

One of my spiritual children, Rich, often said to me, "Frances, I don't believe the Lord intends for you to work yourself to death in the office the way you're doing!" I told him I had to make a living, and there was nothing I could do about it. During the last year, I developed phlebitis in my legs, more acute in the left leg than the right, but I still continued to work. I had gone to the doctor after I discovered I was not praying through for God's healing. I couldn't understand why. The doctor told me to not spend so much time in the office, and to elevate my feet. I still insisted the work had to go on. Now, and only now, do I see how God was dealing with me. Please hold this part of the story in your mind as I continue to another part of the puzzle which slowly began to fit together.

My only son, Tom, to whom this book is dedicated with much love, married an adorable girl when they were both nineteen. Tom was not raised in a Christian home and had absolutely no Christian training. I was a "good" person and tried to teach him to be "good," but this isn't worth much without being a Christian. His daddy had died when Tom was only five, and I had tried to be both mother and father.

No matter how capable we think we are, this is a nearly impossible job for any woman to accomplish, especially without Christ.

Tom has been rebellious throughout the years and I have cried bitter tears over my only son. When the problems with Tom became so great, I took him to a psychiatrist, who said, "If you were an undependable alcoholic Tom would rise up and be a man."

And I always replied: "What can I do? I have to make a living for us and it's too late for me to change. He'll just have to learn to get along with the world, including me." How stupid can a mother be? Pretty stupid, I say, especially when you don't know God well enough to call on him to solve your problems.

In spite of the fact that Tom also is a leader, and in spite of the fact we could really fight with each other, we have an unusual love for each other as well. And even though we have gone through periods of not being able to stand each other, the great love between mother and child was there.

While Tom was in high school, he learned to operate the printing presses and all the equipment in the office, but decided he couldn't work for me because I couldn't let a fifteen-year-old be boss. He went to work for another company before he was married. But eventually he wanted to come back and work for my company which had grown rapidly and which I had always planned to leave to my two children when I died.

Three years ago he came back to work for me. And in spite of loving each other, we managed to ruffle each other's feathers endlessly. Because I had become a Christian, I tried to win him with God's love, but did not succeed. We had constant bickering and dissension in the office. I continued to work ridiculous hours because he continued to goof off and the situation seemed to get worse and worse. I fired him innumerable times but he always came back to work saying he "couldn't do that to me!"

Tom and his wife have had difficulties through the years but somehow they seemed determined to stay together. After four years the Lord blessed them with an adorable son, but even this wasn't enough to keep the marriage on an even keel.

I became involved in this situation and because I wouldn't lie for him, Tom became enraged at me and came to the apartment where my daughter and I live. He declared I wasn't his mother, that he was disowning me, that he couldn't stand either his sister or me, and that he was never going to forgive me as long as he lived. While this went on all I did was sit there and pray for him. The situation was so tense my daughter was crying. My heart just ached, but it seemed God just wanted me to keep still, and so I did.

After Tom left that night, my daughter and I prayed some of the most anguished prayers of our lives. I have prayed continually for my son ever since I became a Christian. Each time he has come so close my heart has thrilled, and then I have seen him back away. Perhaps I never really gave him totally to God, because each time I took my prayer burden back to my own heart and tried to solve it myself.

Well, that night I guess for the first time I completely surrendered my son to God. I cried out in the greatest agony I had ever experienced and said "God, I don't care what the price is, I'll pay it. But make a man out of my son. Lord, somehow reveal to me what must be done in this situation. I don't care what it is." I begged, I pleaded, I cried and then I was exhausted. But in the exhaustion came the peace of God because I knew that I had at last released my son to God.

When I began accepting speaking engagements, I made a practice of calling home daily to solve all the problems in the office, to iron out the little details. Right at the time of this great mother-son battle I had scheduled three big trips right in succession. The first trip I went on might have created some apprehension on my part, but it didn't because I was secure in the knowledge that I had given my son to God, and so I left on my tour. Now see what God did!

This trip was to a church where the pastor is an outstanding Christian psychologist. At the time I accepted the invitation to his church, I was not aware of this fact. But God knew.

I had gone to the church on Saturday night for a banquet, and after we went to the pastor's home for the night, this pastor made mention of his Christian marriage counseling. I immediately took note and just briefly told him about my son and his wife. I had prayed less than one week before this for the Lord to send me the answer and here a man of God was ready to listen and help me with this problem.

We sat up until about 3 A.M. as he explained in language a layman could understand why a problem existed in our family. But it ended up with a clearcut decision when he said: "Frances, you're not a domineering mother, but you're an overwhelming mother, and that's the whole problem!"

I felt like I had been kicked in the stomach. I had wanted to find out what was wrong with my son. Instead I learned he only wanted to be a *man*, but because of an overwhelming mother, he couldn't be. So he had to fight back at me—in spite of loving me—by being rebellious and doing things he knew I didn't approve of.

I had prayed that God would give me the answer or show me the problem, and he did, but it certainly wasn't what I expected. I asked the minister psychologist what I could do about the situation, and he said, "Let's talk to God and see what he says." I went to bed that night and prayed that God would reveal to me through this man the answer to my problem. And he did! The next morning we all got up early for breakfast. As we sat down to eat, the pastor's words seared into my very soul. He said, "Frances, God spoke to me last night and told me what to tell you to do." We formed a prayer circle around his kitchen table. He said, "*You're* Tom's whole problem. He wants to be a man, and he can't be until you walk out of that business and leave it to him with no strings attached."

I said, "But *everything* I own is in that business, even the money from my house which I sold. And years of hard, *hard* work. I have absolutely nothing else!" (We had just enlarged and I had put all my house money into the business.)

He said, "Frances, do you really trust God? Do you really believe he will supply your every need? Do you have faith to believe that you have nothing to fear?"

I admitted that I do trust God, but I believe with all the strength in my body that he will supply my every need, and believe that I have nothing to fear. And then I started crying. All the emotion I had felt concerning the problem just spilled over. That cry lasted almost until we were due at the morning church service. The pastor told me, "You've got to go back and tell Tom you want out to do the things God has called you to do. Tell him you're giving him the business and if it goes bankrupt, it will just have to go bankrupt, because God has called you for a special purpose." For one brief moment I swallowed real hard, then turned my back on everything I had worked to accomplish. Finally I said, "Praise the Lord." I knew that in the total surrender of my problem God had furnished its solution. We prayed that morning that God would supply my needs as I made the decision to turn my back on everything I possessed. I now was, at the age of fifty-three, the owner of only one thing, an automobile.

Immediately before the church service, the pastor

asked me if I really believed God would supply my every need. I assured him that I did, and he said, "Well, we're going to test your faith this morning. We're going to ask the congregation for a $300 love offering for you." This, I knew, was a tremendous amount for a love offering, but I swallowed hard and said yes when he asked me if I believed that God would supply it.

The service was beautiful. Possibly because we had all been under such a deep emotional strain, we were totally submissive to God. When the service was over, the ushers came up and reported the love offering amounted to $300.05. God had very deliberately and very carefully honored faith and had proven himself. I thought of the words in Malachi, "Prove me . . . if I will not open you the windows of heaven and pour you out a blessing, that there shall not be room enough to receive it." We had proven God. Or had God proven himself to us?

I flew home and the first words I said to my son were: "I'm tired of this business, do you want it? If so, you can have it. I'm too old for all this, and I want to do what God has called me to do." I haven't been to work on time since, and I don't go in very often. The day Tom hired the last person needed to replace me, my heart slightly skipped a beat, but I knew I had listened as God had spoken.

The Lord knows how difficult it is for a leader to no longer be the leader, so he promptly sent me on another tour. Instead of calling the office each day to solve all the problems, I carefully refrained from calling even once. Every time I was tempted, God reminded me not to forget his answer, and to stop trying to clutch the problem back to myself. Finally, after ten days, my son caught up with me by phone and told me about a problem and asked my advice. I knew the answer immediately, but God's Holy Spirit nudged me, and instead of giving him a solution I said, "I don't know, honey, I'm here and you're there. So you'll have to solve it yourself."

I continued on one of the most fabulous trips of my life with no more concern for my office. I knew God was handling the situation far better than I could or had ever handled it. Following this trip I went back to the office for a few days, trying only to pick up some of the loose ends of the business. Finally aware how much smarter God is than I am, off I went on another tour, and, with just a few days in between, still another tour.

I can only share with you that the most interesting things have happened! All of a sudden, my "goof-off" son is working half the night just like his mother used to, to keep customers happy. All of a sudden the irresponsible young man has become a dependable young man.

As I watch this interesting puzzle with all its pieces fitted into place, I can only marvel at how many prayers God has answered all at one time. But how long it took for all these pieces to go together, all because I wouldn't listen when God said, "Let me do it my way."

First of all, in a previous chapter I mentioned the fact that I thought God wanted me to sell my business, because he had put such a great call on my life. I knew that he wanted all of my energy for his work, and yet I had not heard what he was telling me—that he wanted me *totally* dependent upon him. He didn't respond to the fleece I threw out, because he didn't want me to *sell* my business.

And you may recall my saying I knew God had a special reason for my selling my house. I didn't know why at the time, but now I do. First of all, so that I wouldn't be tied to a worldly possession. And, second, so that the money would be put into enlarging my business, again making me *totally* dependent upon God.

A year ago, from too many working hours, my left leg was so full of fire and pain and fever I was ready for anything. I think I even would have consented to letting it be amputated. Finally on Thanksgiving Eve my doctor made arrangements to put me in the hospital, because the pain was unbearable. Since I wes scheduled to speak at a Youth Convention on Thanksgiving Day, I called and said I wouldn't be able to be there.

After the Thanksgiving Eve service at our church, three pastors came to see me at home, all standing at the foot of my bed. Instead of placing their hands on my head as they usually do, my own pastor held onto my big toe while they prayed that God would not send me to the hospital, but to the Youth Convention where I belonged.

At six o'clock the next morning I got a call from my doctor (who is also my spiritual son). He wanted to know how my leg felt. *The fever was gone and so was the pain!* Then he told me he had slipped out of his bed at midnight and prayed that God would give him the wisdom to know what to do concerning my leg problem. He prayed that God would make it unnecessary for me to go to the hospital.

I told him there was no more fever and no more pain (and to this day the fever and pain have never returned), so he told me not to go to the hospital. Instead, he put me on a daily recall basis to the hospital. He said he would call me back at noontime to see how I was doing.

I prayed the entire morning asking God to let me go to the Youth Convention. By noontime I felt much better and when he called, I got real brave and asked him if I could go to the Youth Convention. He almost went through the roof! Finally he said, "Well, all right. If you have a private room and bath at the Youth Convention, you can go!"

Well, now, that's an impossible situation, isn't it? A Youth Convention is where you *always* get put in a room with thirty other kids! My daughter had gone on ahead in the morning because she was afraid I wouldn't be able to make it. But she called back about three in the afternoon to say, "Mother, I don't know how you rate, but they've got a *private* room for you."

I said, "Thank you, Lord," because I knew where God wanted me. I got up and dressed and went to the youth convention.

Many people just don't believe in the power of God, don't believe what the Bible says, don't believe that God can heal today just like Christ did 2,000 years ago. I *know* that he can, but to please my family I went to a cardiovascular specialist to have tests made to find out the cause of the problem. After running the gamut in tests, the specialist called me back personally to tell me that my tests were fabulous for a person my age. He sent the report to my doctor and a copy to me. It said: "Cause—unknown. Treatment—nothing."

You see, God gave me the assurance that this would not be a critical problem in my life, although I could not understand why I had been unable to pray through on this problem. Now, and only now, do I know. God was telling me to cut out the long hours of work and to get out of a business that could create problems. Yet he assured me he was watching over me.

While my leg is not entirely healed as of the writing of this final chapter, it is so improved it's almost unbelievable. And every morning when I awaken and look at my legs I say, "Well, praise the Lord, for all things work together for good for those who love the Lord. And, Lord, I just can't wait to see the miracle which will come about as a result of this leg problem."

One of the miracles is that God was telling me to do it his way, to leave behind a business that sapped my energy, my strength, my very being. Even now as I write this, most of my friends do not know the decision I have made. Yet I didn't make it. I asked God to reveal to me his Perfect Will for my life and he did, so there was no question of a decision, only a question of being obedient to his will.

Right now I don't know exactly what God wants for my life. I do know that as long as I stay in tune with his Holy Spirit, he will lead me day by day, moment by moment. If anyone had told me four years ago—or even one short year ago—that I would ever leave this business into which I poured my very soul, I would have never believed it. Yet, because I have learned to "abide," God has prepared my heart with never a desire to look back, but to anticipate the exciting future he has for me.

As for my son, Tom, I don't know what God has planned for his life. I only know that in surrendering him completely to God's care, my worry is gone. Never have I been so free as I am right now. Never have I ever anticipated the future with as much excitement as I do right now. I'm sure that God knows what he wants from my life, and I'm equally sure that because he plans it, it will be the most fabulous part of my life.

Am I worried or concerned over the future? No! God's Word says not to worry about a thing. Do I believe it? Yes, I do. Of the few persons who know of the decision, one said, "Aren't you afraid or nervous because of your age?" No, I'm not afraid, because *God knows how old I am.* I reminded this friend of a magnificent verse in Mark, chapter 4, where the great storm of wind arose, and the disciples got shook up. Christ said, "Why are you afraid? Have you no faith?"

I'm not afraid because I have faith to believe in God's holy word. And I have faith to believe that God answers prayer and in answering one little prayer, he answered a lot of great big prayers. And I also know that now I am FREE.

And so this book is dedicated to Tom with all of his mother's love, because it was through my heartache over him that God gave me the greatest victory of my life. I shed the snake-skin sin of holding on to him and, in so doing, learned the real meaning of total surrender. Thank you, my son, for being the one God used to make me know unmistakably that, for any Christian, prayer is a hot line to heaven.